SLR Photography

SLR Photography

A Handbook of the Single Lens Reflex

Derek Watkins

David & Charles

Newton Abbot · London · North Pomfret (Vt) · Vancouver

For my wife, Jill, who was an FP4 widow during
the spring and summer of 1974

ISBN 0 7153 7301 3

Library of Congress Catalog Card Number 76 - 54090

© Derek Watkins 1976

Set in 9pt on 10pt Linotype Helvetica by Trade Linotype Limited
and printed in Great Britain
by Biddles Limited   Guildford   Surrey
for David & Charles (Publishers) Limited
Brunel House   Newton Abbot   Devon

Published in the United States of America
by David and Charles Inc
North Pomfret   Vermont   05053   USA

Published in Canada
by Douglas David & Charles Limited
1875 Welch Street North   Vancouver   BC

Contents

Introduction

The single lens reflex, or SLR as it is commonly known, is the most popular type of camera currently available. There are several reasons for this. In the first place it is an easy camera to use, because what you see through the viewfinder you record on the film; and what is sharp in the viewfinder will be sharp on the film. Secondly, it is a very versatile camera. Lenses of a wide variety of focal lengths are available for it, as are close-up attachments, microscope adapters, motor drives, astronomical telescope adapters, and so on. So the SLR can be quickly changed from a general purpose camera into an instrument capable of tackling many highly specialised branches of photography.

Although the SLR is very much a camera of today, it is by no means a new camera in principle. As long ago as 1861 a British patent was in existence for a single lens reflex, and in 1888 a system that moved the mirror out of the light path before the exposure was patented. But the modern SLR has come a long way since then, with its fast lenses, through-the-lens exposure metering, and wide range of attachments.

This book takes an essentially practical line, showing you how to get the best out of your SLR. Although one chapter in particular contains a number of mathematical formulas, they are there to help you understand the techniques better.

The book is divided into three parts. The first deals with the equipment – cameras, lenses, filters – and how to use them. Then comes a section on picture making. I have taken a few subjects that appeal to a large number of photographers and given such advice as I have found has helped me. Finally there is a section on techniques: how to use an exposure meter to the best advantage, choosing and using films, colour and printing.

The book is not, I hope, a mere re-presentation of advice which has been published many times before in other books; it is rather practical advice taken from my own experiences, my successes and my failures over a period of more than 20 years. You may find that some of this advice does not agree with what other writers have said, and some of it may appear to be in direct conflict. But, as I have said, the advice I have given is taken from practical experience and I hope that it enables you to get more from this wonderful hobby of photography.

D.W.

Part 1 SLR Equipment

The Modern SLR

There is no such thing as the universal camera, ideal for every photographic job, but the modern single lens reflex is so versatile that it comes very close to satisfying the description. No other camera is suitable for such a wide range of subjects, and some could not be tackled successfully by any other type. This is almost certainly why the single lens reflex is the most popular type of camera in use today.

SLR Construction

The basic SLR principle is that light reflected from the subject enters the camera through the lens, which focuses it on the film plane. In front of the film plane, at 45° to the path of the light (or the axis of the lens), lies a mirror that turns the light through 90° on to a ground-glass screen in the top of the camera. This screen is exactly the same distance from the mirror as is the film plane, so that everything that would be in focus on the film is also in focus on the ground-glass screen. If you focus the image of your subject, therefore, on the screen, then remove the mirror from the light path, the image at the film plane will be accurately in focus. The mirror in an SLR is pivoted, usually at the top, to allow it to swing out of the light path and cover the ground-glass screen, and so prevent light entering and fogging the film when the shutter opens.

Obviously it is necessary to have a special type of shutter for the single lens reflex, either one which is immediately in front of the film – called a focal-plane shutter – or a between-lens shutter with a device to allow it to stay open for focusing. Most SLR manufacturers take the former course of action, since it enables additional lenses to be produced much less expensively; if the camera has a between-lens shutter, every additional lens must have its own integral shutter. Nevertheless, some SLR manufacturers prefer the between-lens shutter, because they believe it to be more reliable than the focal plane type and because it allows flash synchronisation at all shutter speeds. The Hasselblad is perhaps the most famous SLR using this type of shutter. On the other hand the use of a focal-plane shutter means that the camera will accept a wider range of lenses, especially extreme wide angle and telephoto lenses. But whichever type of shutter is used, the reflex mirror has to be swung out of the light path before the shutter can open. The shutter release, therefore, operates in three stages: first it works a lever that stops the lens down to the taking aperture, then it trips the mirror, and finally it releases the shutter. Most modern SLRs have instant return mirrors and lenses, so that, immediately after the film has been exposed, the picture reappears in the viewfinder at full brightness.

Early SLRs, and some of the larger format models available today, have just the plain focusing screen in the top of the camera, surrounded by a hood to keep out extraneous light. This type of viewfinder works perfectly well but has two big disadvantages: the image, while being right way up, is reversed left to right, and this is a real nuisance when you are trying to take action pictures; and when you want to turn the camera on its side to use a vertical format, you have to go through all sorts of difficult contortions to view the image. This does not, of course, apply to 6 x 6cm SLRs, which you use in the same position for all shots.

As you can imagine, these disadvantages told against the single lens reflex in its early days, but nowadays it is fitted with a rectifying device called a pentaprism, which is mounted above the focusing screen and has a viewing window at the back of the camera. The pentaprism takes the laterally reversed image and turns it round again, so that, when you look into the viewfinder, you see the image right way up and right way round. Also included in the viewfinder is a magnifying lens, so that you see the image practically life size as well. Most modern 35mm SLRs are fitted with a fixed pentaprism, but some of the more expensive models have an interchangeable viewfinder system, allowing you to fit them with a pentaprism, a viewfinder hood, or other attachments, and often you can fit any one of a selection of focusing screens, too. Some of these alternative viewing systems are particularly useful if you are taking pictures in situations that make it impossible to look through the viewfinder in the usual way – extreme wide angle shots inside a building, for example, with the camera right up against one wall.

Advantages of the SLR

The biggest advantage the single lens reflex has over the coupled rangefinder camera is that the viewfinder image always shows you exactly what your picture will look like. No matter whether you are using a standard lens, close-up bellows, a fish-eye lens or an extreme telephoto, the image you see on the focusing screen is what you will get on your negative or transparency. The result of this accuracy is that it is much easier to compose your pictures with an SLR than with other cameras, especially when using very wide angle lenses or long telephotos. But not only can you compose your pictures better, you can also see when your subject is sharply focused. You can stop down the lens and see the depth of field visually and accurately, an impossibility with the coupled-rangefinder camera, when you have to rely entirely on the depth of field scale on the lens mount.

Perhaps the most important advantage of viewing your subject through the taking lens is a complete absence of parallax. No matter how good a coupled-rangefinder camera may be (or a twin lens reflex, come to that), and even if it has built-in parallax compensation, there is still a difference in the positions of the taking lens and the viewfinder or viewing lens. Obviously this means that what you see in the viewfinder is slightly different from what the film sees when you make the exposure. When you are taking landscapes or other long shots, this is of no consequence at all, but when you take portraits or close-up pictures, this slight difference in viewpoint can ruin an otherwise good picture.

Absence of parallax and the facility for checking depth of field visually make the single lens reflex the ideal camera for close-up work. The attachments necessary for close focusing, which are quite inexpensive, are available for even the most inexpensive SLR; they will convert the camera instantly into an instrument capable of reproducing a subject at life size or even bigger on the negative. The story is quite different for the coupled-rangefinder camera and the twin lens reflex. Close-up lenses are the only close-up attachments available for most CRFs and TLRs, and they give only a very limited range. Even for that most advanced and expensive of CRF cameras, the Leica, the attachment is a reflex housing which, in effect, converts the Leica into a single lens reflex, and a somewhat inferior SLR to boot! This reflex housing in itself is so expensive that you could buy a complete SLR in the medium price range, with close-up tubes, for about the same sum.

It is fast becoming the general rule for modern SLRs to be fitted with through-the-lens exposure-metering systems, which are particularly useful for close-up work when it is difficult to obtain a sensible reading with a conventional hand-held meter. Moreover, even in normal day-to-day photography such as portraiture and landscape work, TTL metering automatically takes into account any attachments fitted to the lens (teleconverters, correction filters, a polarising filter, and so on). Contrast filters, though, are usually too dense and alter the tonal rendering of objects too much to enable TTL metering to give a really accurate indication; so in this case you should take a reading without the filter and then open up the lens by the recommended number of stops to compensate for the filter. TTL metering can also be the most convenient way to obtain a correct exposure reading if you are using a long telephoto lens. Just as the viewfinder image in an SLR shows you just what will be in your finished picture, so the TTL metering system bases the exposure reading on just that area of view the lens takes in. With a lens of long focal length, therefore, you can base your exposure very accurately on a distant object, particularly if the metering system is of the spot type.

The major contributing factor to the versatility of the single lens reflex is its enormous range of lenses and accessories – far more than for any coupled-rangefinder camera or twin lens reflex. Even the Leica does not have an available lens with a focal length shorter than 21mm, and even with that lens you have to use an auxiliary viewfinder and accept that it will not operate the rangefinder mechanism. The same is true of long telephoto lenses used with the Leica; in fact it is difficult to get lenses of longer focal length than around 135mm for CRF cameras, and if you want to use a lens longer than this with the Leica, you have to fit the reflex housing that was mentioned earlier. With the SLR, however, you can use lenses from a 7mm fish-eye right up to a 1,000mm mirror, and see exactly what you are getting on the negative every time.

In addition to wide ranges of lenses, there are any number of other accessories available for specific jobs – extension tubes and bellows, focusing magnifiers, motor drives, microscope attachments, and so on. With many of the so-called system cameras, such as the Nikon, the Hasselblad, and, in the lower price range, the Praktica and the Pentax, the list is almost interminable, all of which means that the basic SLR can be converted quickly, easily, and in most cases reasonably cheaply, into a specialised camera for any one of many branches of highly technical photography.

The disadvantages of the SLR

After such praise you may wonder why so many manufacturers are still bothering to produce coupled-rangefinder cameras and twin lens reflexes. The answer is, of course, that the SLR has disadvantages as well as advantages.

The CRF is undeniably faster in operation than the SLR, especially in focusing in poor light, for as the light level falls, the focusing screen becomes darker, until it is quite impossible to focus accurately at all. It is also easier to focus accurately with a rangefinder, because there is no ambiguity about two images being superimposed or in line. It is not so easy to see exactly when an image on a ground-glass screen is sharp, for that is an entirely subjective decision, depending on your own judgement; this is particularly noticeable when you are working at or near full aperture, and there is only a shallow depth of focus to mask focusing errors. In modern SLRs, though, this problem has been solved, at least in part, by replacing the plain ground-glass focusing screen fitted to earlier models with a screen incorporating some form of rapid-focusing aid. One such device comprises a circular microprism or split-image rangefinder in the centre of the screen, usually surrounded by a ring of plain ground glass, and a fresnel condenser to make the corners of the screen brighter. The microprism breaks up the image of the subject when it is out of focus but forms a complete image when accurately focused; and the split-image rangefinder brings the two halves of the image together when focused properly. While these devices solve the problem of focusing accurately and quickly, they do not really help a lot in poor light, but that is a problem you have to learn to live with

when using an SLR. But it is a very minor disadvantage when set against all the very big advantages of this type of camera.

It is indisputable that the single lens reflex is a much more complicated camera than the coupled rangefinder. There is the reflex mirror, which has to swing out of the light path before the shutter can open, and the lens has to stop itself down and restore itself to the viewing mode again after the exposure has been made. All these things tend to make the SLR heavier and noisier than the CRF or TLR. Although the extra noise is not usually an important factor – unless you are taking wild-life pictures close to the subject – the vibration set up by the mirror moving can mean that the SLR is difficult to hold completely still at slow shutter speeds. The amount of vibration is, of course, very small, but then it only needs a very small amount to induce camera shake. Speaking for myself, I cannot guarantee to produce shake-free exposures with an SLR at speeds slower than 1/125 second with the standard 50mm lens, and a lot faster with a telephoto. But if you brace the camera against something you should be able to produce good shots down to 1/30 second.

One of the major disadvantages pointed out by critics of the single lens reflex is that the viewfinder image disappears at the instant of exposure. Consequently, if you are taking portraits and the model blinks as you press the shutter release, you will not know until you have processed the film. Personally I do not find this any problem at all, because if I am taking portraits, I always take a series – usually a whole film – and if the subject is a landscape or building, it does not matter anyway. In addition, most modern SLRs are now fitted with an instant return mirror, so that the screen is blacked out only for the duration of the exposure.

Now you know both the advantages and disadvantages of the SLR. For some types of photography, such as photo-reportage, the coupled-rangefinder camera is without doubt a better choice, which explains, at least in part, why so many photo journalists use Leicas. But for most other types of photography, and certainly for the general use to which the amateur puts his camera, the SLR must be preferable if only on the grounds of versatility. To my mind the advantages greatly outweigh the disadvantages. If you have decided on an SLR, therefore, the question now is which one to choose from the dozens available.

Choosing an SLR

Obviously you must first decide how much you can afford to spend and just what you want for that money. Single lens reflexes are now available in all price ranges from less

1 An SLR in the top price bracket – the Nikon F2

2 The Praktica LLC is one of the best lower-priced SLRs

than £30 to over £700, so no matter how much you have to spend, if you are interested in a serious camera, you can afford an SLR. Unless expense really is no object, you are wasting money by buying one of the top-priced SLRs. While the degree of precision with which, say, a Nikon (Illus 1) or a Canon is built is undoubtedly higher than that of a Praktica or a Pentax, the difference is mainly one of toughness. The Nikon and Canon are basically designed for professional use, and will stand up to the hard life of the professional world for many years. Less expensive SLRs are not so rugged, but, for all that, they are not fragile in any way and will give the amateur a lifetime of service with little or no trouble. To underline this point, I use Praktica cameras (Illus 2), and as a freelance photographic journalist I certainly work them hard, as may be seen from the worn paintwork and small dents in the pentaprism housing. One of these cameras, a Prakticamat, has been in use now for well over eight years, and it has never let me down yet.

The optical performance of a top-flight SLR is better than that of a lower-priced camera, but it has been my experience that this difference is marginal; if you were shown a collection of prints or transparencies, some taken with a Nikon and others with a Praktica, I think you would be hard put to pick out which were which. Scientific tests would doubtless show up quite significant differences, but we are interested in the practical use of a camera and lens, not the results of scientific tests.

My advice, therefore, would be to buy an SLR in the medium price range – £70 to £200 in the UK. This would cover such cameras as Praktica, Pentax, Yashica or Mamiya; all of these are system cameras, which means that there are a great many additional lenses and other accessories available for them. Perhaps one of the first pieces of additional equipment you might consider is a second camera body, which in effect gives you two cameras, enabling you to keep black and white in one and colour in the other, or slow film in one and fast in the other. Another alternative is to keep the same type of film in both for a situation where you are shooting rapidly and cannot afford time to reload.

The camera you decide to buy will, of course, be a matter of personal preference, coloured perhaps by what sort of discount you can get off a particular model. Before you part with any money, read all the test reports you can find on the camera of your choice, but do not be put off by small criticisms, for the reviewers have personal preferences, too. If a recurring fault is mentioned, however, or dislike is evident in all or most of the reviews, find out more about the camera – but do not forget that the reading of test reports is no substitute for handling the camera yourself.

Everything I have said about choosing an SLR so far applies equally to 35mm cameras and to larger format SLRs – 6 x 6cm and 6 x 7cm. There are no really inexpensive larger format SLR's, however, and your choice is restricted to about half a dozen cameras.

Your choice of 35mm or a larger size will depend entirely on the type of photography you want to do. If you want to concentrate on taking colour transparencies for publication, your best choice would be a larger format SLR; but for general photography, I would not hesitate in recommending 35mm as the most suitable format, for two very good reasons. Firstly, 35mm SLRs are very much more compact than their bigger brothers, and that means they are lighter and easier to handle; and secondly, 35mm film is considerably cheaper, frame for frame, than the larger film size. The fact that the negative size is smaller is of no great importance these days. Films have improved so much in recent years that it is now possible to produce sharper, more defined images on 35mm film than you could on 6 x 6cm negative format 10 or 12 years ago. I know this to be true because I have a large number of 6 x 6cm negatives I took with a Rollei about 15 years ago, and the prints I can make from these negatives are nothing like the quality of those I can make from my current 35mm negatives. True, I have changed my techniques considerably during the period, but most of the improvement can be laid at the door of better films.

Handling an SLR

The single lens reflex is, as we have already seen, the most versatile camera available today, and there is not much you cannot tackle with at least a reasonable chance of producing successful pictures. But before you can do that, you must learn to handle the camera properly. Even the most advanced and expensive SLR you can buy will not produce superb pictures on its own.

Remember that the camera is only a machine, a tool, a means of enabling you, the photographer, to interpret and record your subject on film – just as an artist's paintbrushes are only tools to enable him to interpret his subject. So, to make the camera record the subject in the way you want to interpret it, you must set the controls correctly.

It is very tempting, when you buy a new camera, to take it out of its box as soon as you get it home, put a film in, and start shooting pictures right away. Resist this temptation. The first thing you must do is read the instruction book from cover to cover with the camera in front of you. I remember once hearing a rather cynical camera repairer saying that most photographers seem to believe in the philosophy, 'When all else fails, try reading the instructions'. Please do not be one of these people. The instruction book is included to help you use the camera to the full without damaging it, so read it sooner rather than later. It will tell you how to load your camera and how to take pictures with it. This chapter is in no way intended to replace the instruction book but merely to give you additional information, advice and practical tips on how to get the best out of your camera.

The three main controls

Before you press the shutter release, you must set three controls correctly if you want the picture to be successful. These controls are focusing, shutter speed, and aperture, and they will, if used properly, enable you to take pictures that are technically good – that is, accurately focused and correctly exposed. Once you have mastered their use, they will give you creative control over your pictures as well, allowing you to emphasise parts of the picture or play them down by throwing them in or out of focus, for example, or to give the feeling of movement by blurring part of the picture. All three of these controls are interdependent to some degree: for instance, the aperture control governs both the exposure and the depth of field (the amount in front of and behind the point of focus that is acceptably sharp).

Focus control Focusing with a single lens reflex is extremely easy. Since you view the subject through the lens that takes the picture, everything you see as sharp in the viewfinder will be sharp on the negative or transparency. Therefore, to focus your SLR, you merely look into the viewfinder and turn the focus control on the lens barrel – usually calibrated in feet and metres – until your subject appears sharp. This is usually made even easier by a built-in split-image rangefinder or microprism device in the centre of the focusing screen. But there is slightly more to it than this: to find the exact point of focus, it is generally necessary to adjust the focus control until the image becomes slightly unsharp and then go back to the point of sharp focus again. With rangefinder and microprism, however, this procedure takes little time, and with a little practice can be almost instantaneous.

Another factor which makes focusing easier

is that, with automatic lenses at least, you always focus with the lens at full aperture. This has two advantages: firstly, the screen is comparatively bright, and secondly the depth of field is always shallower at large apertures, so that the image snaps in and out of focus much more noticeably. Even if the lens you are using is not an automatic one, it is likely to have a pre-set diaphragm, which still enables you to focus at full aperture before stopping down to a pre-selected stop.

With many subjects it is necessary only to know that the main focal point of the picture is in focus, but with others, such as landscapes with both foreground and background interest, you need to know how much of the subject is in focus. In other words, you want to know the depth of field. When using a hand camera other than an SLR, you have to depend solely on the depth of field scales on the lens, but with the single lens reflex you can stop the lens down and check the depth of field visually. Since depth of field is so tied in with aperture, we will come back to it a little later when we have looked at the other two controls.

While focusing correctly is quite easy when the subject is obliging enough to keep still, it becomes rather more difficult when the subject is moving, especially if your SLR has a plain ground-glass focusing screen. The trick is to pre-focus on a point where you know or anticipate that the moving subject will pass. Then, when the subject reaches this point, press the shutter release. Do not try to focus on the moving subject, because, by the time you get it all together, chances are the subject will be long gone. If you stop the lens down to f/8 or so, the depth of field will take care of any slight delay or anticipation in releasing the shutter.

Shutter speed control The shutter speed control governs the length of time for which the image-forming light entering the camera is allowed to act on the film. So, together with the aperture setting, it controls the exposure. But it also has another important purpose: it enables you to control whether your subject is sharp or blurred. In this way you can create a sense of movement in your picture or freeze the motion to give a moment in time suspended for ever. The shutter is calibrated in fractions of a second from one second to 1/500 or 1/1,000 second, each speed being approximately half the speed of the preceding one. In addition, there is usually a B setting, which keeps the shutter open all the time you are pressing the release button. The B stands for bulb, a reminder of the early days of photography when the shutter was opened and closed pneumatically by the photographer squeezing and releasing a rubber bulb.

Obviously, when the subject you are photographing is moving in front of the camera, it will produce an image that moves across the film while the shutter is open. The result will be a blurred image on the negative, and the slower the shutter speed the greater will be the degree of blur. But the amount of blur also depends on the camera to subject distance, the focal length of the lens you are using, and the angle to the camera at which the subject is moving. The first two factors – distance and focal length – both determine the size of the image on the negative, and this in turn determines the degree of blur, because the larger the image at the film plane the faster this image moves across the film.

A moving object always appears to be moving faster if it is passing at right-angles to your line of sight than if it is moving at a smaller angle or coming towards you, so that you need a faster shutter speed to stop the motion of an object passing directly across your path. For example, if you need a speed of 1/500 second to stop a subject moving at right-angles to you, you need half this speed, 1/250 second, to freeze motion if the subject is moving at 45° to you. Table 1 gives you a guide to which shutter speed to use to stop movement at various speeds and angles.

Table 1   Shutter Speeds

Subject	Dist(ft)	Direction of movement		
		0°	45°	90°
People walking,	10	1/125	1/250	1/500
children playing,	20	1/60	1/125	1/250
boats, waves, etc	50	1/30	1/60	1/125
Ball games,	10	1/500	1/1000	—
running, motor-	20	1/250	1/500	1/1000
boats, horse	50	1/125	1/250	1/500
racing, traffic in				
towns, etc				
Racing cars,	20	1/500	1/1000	—
express trains,	50	1/250	1/500	1/1000
aeroplanes, etc	100	1/125	1/250	1/500

You will notice that there are two positions in Table 1 in which no shutter speeds are indicated. This means that, even using the fastest shutter speed on your camera (assuming it is 1/1,000 second), you will still have a blurred image on your negative or transparency. The technique you can use to overcome this problem is called panning. All you do is follow the motion of your subject, keeping it stationary in the picture area, and release the shutter when the subject reaches a predetermined spot. The effect of this is to produce a sharp image of the moving object against a blurred background, which also helps to convey the impression of speed. You can vary the amount of blurring in the background by carefully choosing the shutter speed you use; with practice it is possible to pan at speeds as low as 1/125 second or even slower.

The real art of panning lies in a smooth flowing movement of your body, continued after you have released the shutter, rather like a golfer following through on a shot. Stand with your feet well apart and swing your body from the hips; practise the movement a few times and you will soon be producing perfectly panned shots every time.

Aperture control The aperture control on your SLR is important, for it influences the effects of both the other two controls. It influences exposure, because it controls the brightness of the light entering the camera; and it influences focus, because it controls how much of the subject is reproduced sharply.

If you want to take a picture at a particular shutter speed – perhaps the subject is moving and this governs the speed you use – the only way you can achieve the correct exposure is by setting the aperture control at the f/number indicated by your meter for that shutter speed. How the aperture works is described in Chapter 3, so suffice it to say here that the control is marked with a series of numbers – 4, 5.6, 8, 11, and so on – which are called stops. If you move the control from one f/number to the next larger number, you will halve the amount of light entering the camera; if you move the control to the next smaller number, you will double the amount of light entering the camera.

While controlling the brightness of the light reaching the film is the fundamental job of the aperture, its effect on the sharpness of the image is equally important. If you focus on an object 10ft in front of your camera, and make your exposure with the lens at full aperture, you will find that, while the object on which you focused is sharp, objects a few feet in front of or behind this object will be out of focus. If you now repeat the exposure, but with the lens stopped down to f/8 or so, you will find that some of the objects that were out of focus in the first shot are now sharply reproduced. The further you stop the lens down, the further in front of and behind the point on which you have focused will the zone of sharpness extend. This zone, which is called the depth of field, depends on the focal length of the lens and the focused distance, as well as on the lens aperture used.

Depth of field, used properly, can be one of your most useful creative tools in photography. By increasing it you can make the maximum possible depth of objects in your picture sharp, from a few feet, or even inches, in front of the camera to infinity; and by reducing it to the minimum you can make your subject stand out sharply from out-of-focus foreground and background.

Most lenses have a depth of field scale en-graved on the lens barrel in the form of a series of f/numbers on each side of the focusing mark, and this enables you to check how much of your subject will be in focus at any stop you choose. To use it in the simplest way, focus your subject, then read off the nearest and farthest points that will be sharp from the depth of field scale. Of course, you can also carry out a visual check by stopping the lens down to the taking aperture. But the depth of field scale can be used in a much more creative way than this. For example, let us assume that you are taking a picture that demands the greatest possible depth of field right up to infinity. The subject contains moving figures, so that the shutter speed can be no longer than, say, 1/60 second, and at this shutter speed the lighting conditions require an aperture of f/5.6. To obtain the maximum depth of field possible at this aperture, set the infinity mark on the focusing scale to the f/5.6 mark on the depth of field scale, then, if you look at the f/5.6 mark on the other side of the focusing mark, you will see that the nearest sharp point of the subject is indicated. With a 50mm lens, the distance at which the lens will be focused is about 30ft and the closest point in sharp focus is about 20ft.

The depth of field scale also helps you to have your camera ready at all times for those unexpected pictures that sometimes crop up. If you take an exposure reading when you go out and set the shutter speed and aperture controls, you will be ready. But if the unexpected does happen, you will not have time to focus. Set the focus control, therefore, in conjunction with the depth of field scale, so that the zone of sharpness extends over the most likely area of action – for example, from 12–50ft for shots in the street. Now if you see something that could make an interesting picture, you can shoot first and refocus more accurately for a second shot if there is time; if not, well at least you have an acceptable picture.

You can also make use of the aperture control to give you minimum depth of field, which will enable you to focus selectively on the most important part of the subject, throwing the rest out of focus. This, which is done by simply using the lens at or near full aperture, is a valuable creative tool, enabling you to emphasise one particular part of your subject while relegating other parts to soft fuzzy shapes.

Aperture and shutter speed combined We have seen how both the shutter speed and the aperture control the exposure you give a subject: the aperture governs the brightness of the light that falls on the film and the shutter speed the length of time for which this light acts. The combination of aperture and shutter speed, therefore, determines the degree to which the emulsion of the film is affected by light – in other words, the exposure. Since any stop on your lens allows twice the amount of usable light to pass as the next higher f/number, as do increases on the shutter speed scale, it is obvious that you can use several combinations of these two controls to give you the same exposure. For instance, 1/30 second at f/16 will give the same exposure as 1/250 second at f/5.6, 1/500 second at f/4, or 1/15 second at f/22. The range of these combinations is determined by the brightness of the light reflected from the subject and the speed of the film in your camera.

Just which particular combination of shutter speed and aperture you use will depend on the type of subject you are photographing and the effect you want. By using a slow shutter speed and small aperture you can produce great depth of field, but movement will be blurred. This combination is therefore unlikely to be suitable for photographing sport, but it would be ideal for still-life or close-up pictures of, say, flowers. On the other hand a fast shutter speed and large aperture will give you shallow depth of field but will freeze all but the fastest action. Between these two extremes there are several other combinations you can use to give you degrees of depth of field and stopped movement.

You have now looked through the viewfinder, focused your subject, taken a meter reading, set the shutter speed and aperture controls to give you the result you want, composed your picture and checked the depth of field. You are now ready to take your picture, and face the most critical part of the procedure – pressing the shutter release. More pictures are spoiled at this point than anywhere else along the line. The reason is camera shake, which is caused by not holding the camera steady when you press the button, or by jabbing the shutter release instead of squeezing it.

Holding your SLR

One of the big advantages, and disadvantages, of the 35mm SLR is that it is relatively small and light. Because it is so small and light, it is difficult to hold perfectly still; the slightest movement, even the very action of pressing the shutter release, is enough to cause it to waver unless you take precautions to prevent it from doing so.

Ideally the camera should be fixed to a firm tripod for every exposure, but, as this is often impracticable, you must do the next best thing – make yourself into a rigid support for the camera (Illus 3-5). This is relatively easy to do in most situations. If you are standing to take the picture, plant your feet firmly 2–3ft

apart, making sure that they are on a solid foundation. Hold the camera up to your eye and tuck your elbows well into your sides; if the camera has a strap (which it should have), take a turn of it round your wrist so that it pulls tight across the back of your neck to give an extra anchorage point. Use your right hand to hold the camera and support it with your left hand under the lens. This position enables you to use the thumb and index finger of the left hand to operate the focusing and aperture rings, and the index finger of the right hand to release the shutter. I find this stance generally quite comfortable for taking pictures with a horizontal format. For vertical pictures there are two schools of thought about how best to hold the camera. Some recommend you to hold it so that the shutter release button is at the top, with your right hand and arm angled above the camera. Personally I find this position rather uncomfortable and, because the right arm is away from the side of the body, a little unstable. Instead I prefer the alternative where you hold the camera cradled in your right hand, with the left hand supporting the lens as in the horizontal position. In this case you operate the shutter release with the thumb of your right hand. I have found this a much more stable hold, because the elbows are well into the sides of the body.

If you are using a shutter speed slower than 1/60 second, you will find it difficult to hold an SLR completely still, and it is advisable to find some sort of supplementary support. As an alternative to a tripod you can lean against a wall or tree, or rest the camera on top of a gate. But if none of these are available, you can always sit on the ground, resting your elbows on your knees for extra support.

All these notes on holding a camera apply to short focal length lenses and medium telephotos up to about 135mm. Above this focal length it is extremely difficult to keep the camera steady enough to avoid camera shake, even at shutter speeds of 1/250 second or even faster, because the object you are photographing is magnified and any shake is magnified by the same factor. Therefore, it is almost essential to use a tripod when working with these longer lenses, and when using shorter lenses at slow shutter speeds.

How to hold your SLR:
3 In the horizontal position

4 In the vertical position

6 How to hold an SLR with a long telephoto lens fitted. The left hand supports the heavy lens while the right hand balances the camera. But always use your camera on a tripod if possible when working with a long lens

5 An alternative and, in my opinion, preferable vertical hold. Note the position of the arms and feet in these stances. If there is a convenient wall or tree trunk, lean on it to give yourself added stability

Making the exposure The action of pressing the shutter release is extremely important if you are to avoid camera shake. If you merely jab at the release, you are almost certain to move the camera and get a blurred image. The trick is to squeeze the release *very gently*, rather like you would squeeze the trigger if you were firing a rifle. Practise a few times with an empty camera and you will begin to know by feel just when the shutter is about to trip, so that you will be able to take up the free movement and release the shutter under perfect control.

When pressing the shutter release with your index finger, place your thumb under the base of the camera. Then, when you operate the release, press up with your thumb at the same time; this gives an equal and opposite force and the camera should remain perfectly steady. When you are holding the camera vertically to release the shutter with your thumb, the same principle applies, but this time the opposite pressure is applied by the fingers.

Looking after your SLR

The single lens reflex is a precision optical and mechanical instrument, and if you want it to give you good results for a number of years, you should treat it as such. As a start, keep your camera clean. When each film has been through the camera, open the back and brush the film channels, pressure plate, cassette chamber and take-up area with a soft camel-hair brush to loosen any particles of dust, grit and emulsion or backing. Then turn the camera upside down and use a small air blower to puff these bits out. This simple cleaning routine will go a long way towards eliminating one of the major problems in 35mm photography – tramline scratches on your negatives or transparencies. Next, unscrew the lens and use your brush and blower around the mirror and focusing screen areas to remove dust and hairs, bits of paint, and so on, which, while not affecting the quality of your pictures, have an annoying habit of settling on the focusing screen just when you are composing them.

Lenses obviously need to be kept clean. You should dust your lens with a soft brush every time you use it, so that it never reaches the state where you will need to do more. Dust on a lens does not affect the sharpness of your pictures very much, unless there is a lot of it, but it does reduce the contrast of the image. Every six months or so it is as well to clean your lens a little more thoroughly. Clean each exposed surface with a *fresh sheet* of special lens-cleaning tissue. Do not be tempted to use a handkerchief, even if it feels very soft, for handkerchiefs can harbour grit, the arch enemy of optical glass, and even if the grit

particle is too small to be seen or even felt, it will not be too small to scratch the delicate surfaces of the lens.

When you are not using a particular lens, always keep the external surfaces covered with lens caps to prevent accidental damage; and when you clean the lens, brush inside the lens cap, too. It is surprising how much dust collects in there before transferring itself to the lens surfaces.

One golden rule about lenses. Never take a lens apart to clean the internal surfaces. Apart from the fact that they should never need cleaning, because it should be impossible for dirt to get inside, stripping a lens down is a highly specialised job. It needs complex optical equipment to make sure that the reassembly work is carried out properly, and without this equipment it is virtually impossible to restore the lens to its former capability.

Cameras have two great enemies – sand and moisture. It is fairly simple to protect your camera against sand by keeping it in a tightly closed polythene bag when you take it on to the beach; but it is not so easy to keep moisture at bay, because all sorts of unexpected places become damp at times, and this can play havoc with your equipment. If you leave a film in the camera, damp can quite easily start a fungoid growth on the emulsion, and if the place where you keep your camera is warm as well as damp, the trouble can be even worse. Probably the most satisfactory way of keeping your camera free from damp, apart from storing it in a warm dry place, is to put a small bag of silica gel in the gadget bag or cupboard with it. Silica gel is a desiccant, that is to say it has the property of absorbing moisture very easily and therefore keeps it away from where it can do damage. Since it absorbs moisture, the silica gel needs to be dried out periodically by placing it in a warm oven for an hour or so.

The other major problem caused by damp is, of course, rust. Shutter and diaphragm mechanisms are lubricated only lightly to avoid oil mist inside the camera when they operate, so these delicate metal parts are not very well protected against rust. This is another important reason for making certain your camera does not become damp.

If you need to take pictures in the rain, keep your camera dry by placing it inside a polythene bag sealed with a wire tie. Make a hole for the lens and fix the polythene to your lens hood with Scotch tape. Now, if you have an ultra-violet filter on, the lens is protected as well as the camera itself, and a filter is much cheaper to replace than a lens. (This is not to say, incidentally, that I recommend keeping a filter on the lens at all times. In fact, I recommend *not* using one unless it is essential.) With the camera wrapped up you can go out in the foulest weather secure in the knowledge that it will stay dry. You can operate the controls through the polythene bag, which you should also find transparent enough to allow for viewfinding and focusing.

Of all forms of moisture, salt water is the most insidious by far. If you are using your camera by the sea and it gets splashed, wipe off the salt water immediately. Always keep a filter on to prevent sea-water splashes reaching the lens. Should you have the misfortune to drop your camera in the sea, drastic measures are necessary. First, hold the camera under a fast flowing cold water tap for a few minutes, then place the camera in a bowl of water and leave it to soak for twenty minutes or so to give the clean water time to wash all the salt out of the mechanism. Next, shake as much water out of the camera as possible and dry off all the surface moisture. After that pour some thin machine oil into a tough polythene bag and put the camera in. Slosh the oil around so that it coats all parts of the camera, to prevent rust from setting in. Finally take your camera to a good repairer as quickly as you can and explain to him what has happened. He will be able to degrease all parts, clean them thoroughly, and reassemble the camera. But you will be faced with a big bill!

3 Lenses

Perhaps the biggest single advantage of the single lens reflex is that a vast range of lenses from extreme wide angle to extreme telephoto may be used with the camera body, and all the time you can see exactly what is in your picture through the viewfinder. No other type of camera allows you to do this with such ease. Most SLRs have a range of lenses made for them by the camera manufacturer, and many, especially those with the Praktica/Pentax screw thread system, have several other ranges available from independent manufacturers. Some of these independent lenses have interchangeable mounts, which enable them to be used on several cameras with different lens fittings.

As far as most photographers are concerned, lenses fall into three basic groups – normal, wide angle and telephoto. These terms are, of course, relative, so first perhaps I had better explain what is meant by them.

The whole concept of interchangeable lenses is based on focal length – the distance between the optical centre of the lens and the film plane when the lens is focused on a very distant object (usually referred to as infinity). This distance is expressed in millimetres or, less commonly now, in inches. A lens that is 100mm away from the film plane when focused on infinity is said to have a focal length of 100mm. This is oversimplifying things a little, because some lenses of very long or very short focal length are of special design to make their use practical with SLRs. So-called normal or standard lenses are usually of a focal length roughly equal to the diagonal of the negative format. On a full frame 35mm camera the negative size is 24 x 36mm and the diagonal of this is 45mm. One or two SLRs are available with a 45mm standard lens, but most manufacturers have gone for something a little longer, 50mm and 55mm being the two most popular focal lengths. The reason for choosing a focal length of 45–55mm as standard is that the angle of view, and therefore the apparent perspective produced, are more or less the same as that of the human eye.

Having established what is meant by a normal or standard lens, it is fairly easy to say that, for 35mm SLRs, lenses with focal lengths shorter than 45–55mm are wide angle and those with focal length longer than this are telephoto or, in many cases more correctly, long focus. Wide angle lenses are generally available with focal lengths of anything from 20mm to 35mm, and long focus or telephoto lenses from 85mm up to 1000mm. In addition, there are special-effect lenses known as fish-eye lenses that have focal lengths of 6–17mm, and produce an image with curved perspective and an extremely wide angle of view.

Larger format SLRs have standard lenses of longer focal length. For example, 6 x 6cm cameras have a standard lens of 75–80mm focal length, and for the newer 6 x 7cm format, 90–100mm is the standard focal length.

The focal length of a lens determines three important characteristics of your picture. These are the perspective effect, the scale or image size, and the depth of field.

Perspective and scale

Perspective is a fundamental part of every picture you take, and it is one of the most widely misunderstood terms in photography. The dictionary defines perspective as 'the art of drawing [or in our case photographing] so as to give the effect of solidity and relative distance and size'. More simply, perspective

The effects of different lenses from the same view-point:

7 500mm

implies reproducing a three-dimensional object on a flat sheet of paper so that it retains the effect of depth. This effect is conveyed by the relative sizes of objects in the picture. For example, the front of a building is represented by a square that becomes progressively smaller the further away it is; the front of a building at twice the distance of another similar building will appear to be half the width and half the height. So you can say that the relative sizes of similar objects within a photograph determine their distances from the camera.

The next point about perspective is the one that is often misunderstood. Perspective depends *only* on viewpoint and on no other factor. The focal length of the lens you use *does not* alter the perspective *unless you move nearer to or further away from your subject.* You can prove this for yourself by taking two pictures, one with your standard lens and one wih a long focus lens, from the same point. When you print the shots, enlarge a section of the picture taken with the standard lens so that the print covers the same part of the subject as that in the long focus shot. You will see that the perspective in both prints is identical. From any fixed viewpoint, therefore, lenses of different focal lengths will give the same perspective.

The lens you use on your camera, then, does not in itself control the perspective in the picture. What it does control is the size of the image of an object within the picture format – the scale of the picture. For instance, a 100mm lens with an angle of view of roughly 23° on a 35mm negative will reproduce an object twice as large as will a 50mm lens at the same distance, because the 50mm lens has an angle of view of some 46°. This is one of the basic characteristics of lenses: the longer the focal length of the lens, the bigger the image of the object on any given negative size. This is what probably first attracts the photographer towards buying additional lenses for his camera. By using a telephoto or long focus lens he can make his subject bigger without having to move nearer to it, and by using a wide angle lens he can include a building in his picture without having to step back. But there is a lot more to choosing lenses than this, as you will see later.

From all this it is fairly obvious that you can produce the effect of a long focus lens by merely enlarging a small portion of the negative taken with your standard lens. This can be a useful standby when there is only one possible viewpoint for a picture and the scale you want needs a lens of focal length between two that you have. You simply take

25

8 300mm   **9** 135mm

10 100mm   **11** 50mm

12 35mm   **13** 23mm

14 20mm   **15** 16mm fish-eye

16 Taken with a 50mm lens

17 Taken with 135mm lens from the same spot as 16

Perspective depends **only** on subject distance, as these photographs show:

18 Part of the 50mm negative enlarged to give the same picture area as the 135mm negative in 17

19 35mm

20 50mm

Three pictures of the same subject taken with different lenses at different distances to show the perspective effects:

21 135mm

the shot with the shorter of the two lenses and enlarge a portion of the negative. But there are, of course, disadvantages. Unless you use a slow film, grain will quickly become a major problem and definition will also suffer; and if you are using colour reversal film, you must mask the transparency down or make an enlarged duplicate.

From what I have said so far you can see that the only way you can *control* the perspective in your picture, to change the relation betwen a foreground object and a background object, is to vary both the focal length of the lens and the camera-to-subject distance. You must first establish the relation of foreground to background that you want by moving closer to or further away from the subject. Then you must choose a lens of suitable focal length to include the amount of the subject you want. In this way you can make the perspective in your picture appear steeper or flatter at will.

Distortion The only way you can take a completely distortion-free picture is by having the film plane of your camera parallel with the subject. If you photograph the front of a building head on, the picture will be free from distortion; but if you move slightly to one side, so that the back of the camera is no longer parallel with the building, you bring depth into the picture, and the building will appear to be distorted because the horizontal lines in it will converge. If these lines were continued they would eventually meet at a point on the horizon known as the vanishing point, for there is a vanishing point for all parallel lines lying in the same plane.

If the film plane of your camera is held absolutely vertical when taking an open landscape, the horizon will be exactly in the centre of the picture, and the point on any object in the picture that is on the same level as the horizon will be at the same height as the camera lens. In other words, if you are using your SLR at eye level, and your eyes are 5ft above the ground, all points 5ft high in the picture will be on the same level as the horizon.

While the eye accepts the distortion of converging horizontals as perfectly normal, it refuses to accept that perspective works in a vertical plane as well. If you show a picture of a building with converging *verticals* to anyone, he will immediately say that the building appears to be leaning over backwards. Yet this is an equally normal and natural phenomenon. If you look up at a building, the distance between your eyes and the top of the building is greater than that between your eyes and the bottom of the building. Since an object at a greater distance appears smaller than a similar object at a shorter distance, the top of the

building must – and does – appear to be narrower than the bottom; but your brain corrects for it, because it knows that the sides of the building are parallel. When you take a photograph of a building with the camera tilted upwards, the camera sees the building in exactly the same way as your eyes, but in this case there is no brain to correct it, and the negative shows the verticals on the building as converging. The moral, of course, is not to tilt the camera upwards, but this is unavoidable if you cannot move back far enough to include the full height of the subject with the film plane vertical. Unless you have a perspective control lens, the only thing you can do in a case like this is to correct the converging verticals when you make the print (see Chapter 11, p 00).

The perspective control lens is a specially designed lens in which the optical axis can be moved horizontally or vertically, to include the tops of buildings, for example, while eliminating unwanted foreground. In this way it removes the need to tilt the camera and in doing so eliminates converging verticals. Perspective control lenses are available for only a few cameras, notably the Nikon family, and are usually around 35mm in focal length.

When the focal length of the lens used for a picture is shorter than about 35mm with a 35mm format, the picture tends to look distorted at the edges. This is because the human eye cannot take in an angle of view wider than about 50°–60° without moving, and this is roughly the angle of view of a 35mm lens. The apparent distortion in photographs taken with lenses of shorter focal length than 35mm is caused by the film plane being at right-angles to the optical axis of the lens only at the centre of the picture; at the edges of the negative the angle between the film plane and the optical axis is a long way from a right-angle. As a result, the perspective effect on objects at the edges of the field of view is increased, so that they appear to be elongated.

Depth of field

The other factor in which the focal length of a lens plays a large part is depth of field – the zone in which objects at different distances from the camera are reproduced acceptably sharp in the negative. The way in which focal length controls this is very simple: the shorter the focal length of the lens, the greater will be the depth of field for a given subject distance and aperture.

In any photograph only the point on which the lens is focused will be perfectly sharp, and all objects in front of and behind this point will become progressively less sharp. The two points where this unsharpness becomes unacceptable define the depth of field.

This question of acceptable and unacceptable degrees of unsharpness is the most important factor of all in depth of field, and the limits of definition acceptable to the human eye vary from person to person. Acceptability is based on a phenomenon known as circle of confusion, which is simply the size of a circle the human eye cannot distinguish from a point when both are viewed from a distance of 10in (normal reading distance). The size of this circle for the average person is about 0.01in or 0.24mm.

The circle of confusion is related to the focal length of the lens, and is generally accepted as being 1/1,000 of the focal length; so for a 50mm lens the circle of confusion is 0.05mm. But this is assuming that prints made from your negatives will be viewed at the correct distance – for example, 16in for a 10 × 8in enlargement. Since most people tend to look at prints more closely than this, a circle of confusion of 1/1,500 or even 1/2,000 of the focal length is often used by designers of lenses for 35mm cameras, to allow for the large degrees of magnification necessary from these small negatives.

Obviously, since all interchangeable lenses for an SLR will produce the same size of negative, and since all those negatives will be enlarged to more or less the same size, the rule about circle of confusion being 1/1,000 of the focal length cannot apply. If it did, you would have different standards of acceptable sharpness for lenses of different focal lengths. So it is generally accepted that the circle of confusion calculated for the standard lens (50mm or thereabouts) will be used for all other lenses. This, incidentally, explains why a 135mm lens used with a 35mm camera has a shallower depth of field than the same focal length used on, say, a 5 × 4in technical camera.

Depth of field is also controlled by the camera-to-subject distance (the smaller this distance the shallower the depth of field) and the aperture at which the lens is set (the smaller the stop the greater the depth of field). One point worth remembering is that the depth of field at any aperture is proportional to the focal length of the lens. In other words, the depth of field at f/8 on a 100mm lens is the same as that at f/4 on a 50mm lens.

Diaphragms and Apertures

The amount of light allowed into the camera is controlled by the aperture at which you set the lens, and the aperture is controlled by a device called an iris diaphragm. This is a set of extremely thin metal leaves that are pivoted and connected to a control ring. The leaves are so shaped that they form a circular aperture on the lens axis, and when the control ring is turned, this aperture increases or decreases in size while remaining central. All photographic lenses have the aperture control ring calibrated in a series of numbers, the series universally used now being 1, 1.4, 2, 2.8, 4, 5.6, 8, 11, 16, 22, 32 and so on; these are the stops or f/numbers. Changing from one stop to the next higher number (eg from f/5.6 to f/8) reduces the light transmission by half. Similarly, changing from one stop to the next smaller number doubles the light transmission.

Many lenses have a maximum aperture of f/1.8 or f/3.5 which does not fit in with the standard f/number series. In a case like this all the apertures except the maximum comply with the standard series.

The f/numbers are calculated by dividing the focal length of the lens by the physical diameter of the aperture, so the diameter of any f/number is larger on a long focus lens than it is on a standard or wide angle lens. Strictly speaking, the f/number is accurate only when the lens-to-film-plane distance is equal to the focal length of the lens, or, in other words, when the lens is focused to infinity. But for practical purposes it is regarded as accurate over the normal focusing range of the lens.

Aperture mechanisms One of the drawbacks of the SLR in the early days was its comparative slowness in operation. For focusing to be possible in all but the very brightest of lighting conditions, the lens has to be opened to full aperture. With the early lenses, after you had focused, you had to stop the lens down to the correct aperture manually before making the exposure. While there are still a few lenses of this type available, most now fall into one of two groups – fully automatic and pre-set.

Fully automatic lenses are normally in their wide open position for focusing; you can set the aperture control ring to whatever stop you like, but the lens will remain at full aperture. However, when you press the shutter release, the lens is automatically stopped down to the correct aperture immediately before the shutter operates. This is achieved by a coupling pin in the lens, connected to the aperture mechanism, being pressed by a lever inside the camera body. After the shutter has operated, the lever retracts, releasing the coupling pin, which allows the lens to open to full aperture ready for focusing again.

The other type of lens now in common use is the pre-set type, which has two aperture rings instead of one. One of these rings clicks into the various aperture setting positions and the other turns freely and in fact stops the lens down. When you have determined the correct exposure for your picture, you set the click ring to the correct aperture, and open

up the lens to its full aperture for focusing with the other ring. After focusing, turn the free ring as far as it will go, and this will stop the lens down to the pre-selected stop for the exposure. This type of lens is only a little slower in use than the fully automatic type, and is reliable as long as you remember to turn the stopping-down ring. The big advantage of pre-set lenses is that, because they are much less complicated in construction than the automatic type, they are considerably less expensive. While the professional photographer may reject them on the grounds that they are slightly slower in use and are not foolproof, they are perfectly suitable for the amateur, and their lower cost may mean that you can buy two extra lenses instead of just one.

Choosing and using lenses

Despite the large number of articles that appear regularly in photographic magazines extolling the virtues of wide angle and long focus lenses, for most photographers the standard lens is still probably the most generally useful. It gives scale and perspective similar to the human eye, so that subjects appear normally; and it will usually focus to quite a short distance, which makes it ideal for fairly close work without accessories. But having said this, most SLR users will want to add one or more lenses to their equipment to give it more versatility. The best advice I can give you is to learn how to get the most out of your standard lens before you buy any further lenses, then buy your extra lenses one at a time and learn to use each one properly before you get the next. Try to plan right at the start just what lenses you will eventually want.

Telephoto lenses Most amateur photographers, when they buy their first additional lens, choose a telephoto, probably because telephoto lenses give them a new outlook on everyday subjects. You may wish to produce pictures with flat perspective or take portraits without distortion, or you may be interested in sports or wildlife photography. But unless you know precisely what you want to do with your telephoto, you may end up buying one that is either too long or too short in focal length.

Optically the telephoto lens consists of two groups of elements, the front group being of converging design and the rear group, usually well separated from the front group, of diverging design. The rays of light from the subject are brought together by the front group and spread out again by the rear group. This gives the effect of rays of light reaching the film having converged from a point some distance in front of the lens, which means that

22 The 135mm lens enables you to produce the effect of flat perspective, as in this shot of an old warehouse at Coventry Canal Basin overshadowed by a new block of flats

23 (overleaf) For sports photography a longer focal length lens is useful. A 500mm Pentacon was used for this picture at Silverstone. Note the blurred background caused by panning

the back focus of the lens is considerably shorter than that of a conventional long focus lens, so that the lens can be more compact in construction.

Long focus lenses Once the focal length of a lens becomes longer than around 300mm, the cost of producing telephoto type construction becomes comparatively high, owing to the amount of optical glass needed and the time and skill required to grind and polish the elements. So, for these very long lenses, normal construction is often used, making the lens very long and unwieldly (as long as or longer than its focal length, in fact). A conventional long focus lens, however, uses far fewer elements, often as few as two, compared with perhaps five or six in a telephoto; and with focal lengths as long as 500mm or even 1,000 mm you need to use a tripod anyway, so that the extra length is not too much of an embarrassment.

Mirror lenses An alternative type of construction for lenses of very long focal length is the mirror lens. Lens designers have developed a completely different technique, using curved mirrors instead of transparent glass lenses for some of the elements. Rays of light from the subject enter the lens through corrector elements and travel down the entire length of the lens barrel to a concave mirror. This primary mirror reflects the light back down the lens barrel to the secondary mirror, this time convex, which is mounted in the centre of the front corrector elements and reflects the light back down the barrel yet again. It then passes through conventional glass elements in the centre of the primary mirror, which correct any aberrations that may be introduced by the mirrors. Light transmission is controlled, not by a conventional iris diaphragm, but by neutral density filters placed in the light path between the glass elements at the rear of the lens.

Teleconverters One of the more recent pieces of optical equipment to be introduced to the photographic world is the teleconverter. This is a device that fits between your lens and the camera body, and multiplies the effective focal length of the lens by two or three times; some converters, in fact, are variable and give two, two and a half, and three times multiplications.

The principle of operation is quite simple. The converter, which is a strong negative lens, causes rays of light entering it from the prime lens to diverge and cover an area larger than the negative frame. This means that only the centre part of the image transmitted by the prime lens is used to produce an image at the film plane, and the effect is as though a much longer focal length lens has been used. But while the effective length is increased, the effective aperture of the prime lens is reduced by the same factor: an f/2.8 135mm lens, for example, becomes an f/5.6 270mm lens.

Another drawback is that any faults or aberrations in the prime lens are increased by the same factor as the magnification of the converter, and the sharpness of the lens is reduced by the same amount. However, despite these two apparent disadvantages, teleconverters are, I think, a worthwhile investment if you only need a very long lens occasionally and cannot justify the cost of, say, a 300mm prime lens. If you have a 135mm lens, a 2x converter will give you almost the same results but at a much lower cost. I believe 2x is the most powerful teleconverter that is acceptable, the losses in effective aperture and optical performance being too great with higher powers than this.

The right long lens The focal length of the long lens you buy will obviously depend on the use you want to make of it. One of the main uses of long lenses is in portraiture, where, if you use a standard lens close enough to your sitter to produce a reasonable image size, the face can become distorted through exaggerated perspective: the nose tends to appear larger than it should while the eyes and ears become comparatively small, resulting in a not very flattering picture. If you double the camera-to-sitter distance and the focal length of your lens, you produce a much more satisfactory result, for the distance in depth between the sitter's nose and ears becomes a much smaller proportion of the camera-to-sitter distance, and the perspective becomes flatter, to give a more natural picture. A telephoto of 90mm to 105mm is ideal for portraiture; if you go to a lens much longer than this, the camera-to-subject distance becomes too much for convenience.

As we have seen, although perspective depends solely on camera-to-subject distance, telephoto lenses do appear to give flat perspective, because they produce a small area of a view seen from a great distance. You can use this to your advantage by making it emphasise a pictorial effect. For example, if you are taking a shot of a row of old terraced houses and you want to emphasise the closely packed feeling, you can move to a greater distance so that the perspective becomes flattened and use a long lens to select just the area of the subject you want.

Because of the shallower depth of field, (stop for stop with shorter lenses) produced by telephoto and long focus lenses, you can use differential focus to add impact to your pictures by focusing accurately on the main part of the subject and, using a wide aperture, throw everything else out of focus. The longer the focal length of the lens, the more dramatic this effect becomes.

Probably the most useful all-round focal lengths for pictorial long focus work are 135mm and 180mm. If you want to add a second long lens at a later date, I would suggest 300mm (or buy a 2x converter). If you use a lens with a focal length of 300mm or more, you will almost certainly need to fix the camera and lens to a sturdy tripod to avoid the possibility of camera shake.

Telephoto lenses are widely used in sports photography, not so much for artistic reasons as to bring the subject effectively closer to the camera; they enable you in fact to take close-up pictures of the action from a great distance and in safety. The focal length you use for sports photography depends to a large extent on the sport you are shooting: for example, to take a close-up of a batsman in cricket you will need a much longer lens than to photograph a group of Rugby footballers in a scrum. Generally speaking, though, the most useful range is 300mm to 500mm, which enables you to get a reasonably large image of distant action without being too much of an embarrassment when the action moves closer.

Wildlife photography is where the really long lenses of 500mm and 1,000mm really come into their own. They can save you so much trouble in carrying around hides and other bulky equipment, which would be necessary with shorter lenses; and they can keep you out of danger if you are photographing big game.

Wide angle lenses While the telephoto or long focus lens gives you a new outlook on everyday things, the wide angle, in my opinion, goes a step further – it opens up a whole new way of seeing. It is tempting to look on the wide angle lens simply as a device to enable you to 'get it all in', but it is much more than this. Used properly, it can be a truly creative lens which, with its great depth of field and close focusing characteristics, permits you to place emphasis on a relatively small foreground object while keeping the background in focus to locate, as it were, the subject in its surroundings. It can also be used to introduce deliberate distortion if necessary.

Conventional wide angles The use of straightforward wide angle lenses of normal construction creates problems with SLR cameras because wide angle lenses have short focal lengths and, using normal construction, the rear element of the lens is rather close to the film plane. This in itself does not matter too much, but when you press the shutter release, the lens prevents the mirror swinging out of the way. To overcome this problem, wide angle lenses for use with SLRs are invariably of inverted telephoto or retrofocus design. This simply means that the lens has a longer back focus than one of conventional construction, allowing the lens to be used without fouling the mirror

One of the difficulties in designing and constructing wide angle lenses is retaining even illumination over the whole negative area. All lenses produce a circular image, of which the negative area is just a rectangular portion in the centre. The circular image does not have a sharp edge, with image on one side of it and nothing on the other side, but darkens gradually from the centre of the image to the outside; so that, in all lenses, the centre of the image is brighter than the edges. But because the difference in brightness is very small within the negative area, this does not cause much trouble, except in very wide angle lenses (24mm focal length and shorter), where, in cheaper lenses at least, it can cause vignetting in the corners of the negative. However, by stopping the lens down, the trouble is largely reduced if not eliminated.

Fish-eye wide angles Some 10 years or so ago, a novel type of lens arrived on the photographic scene, and it produced decidedly weird results. Called the fish-eye lens because of its curved protruding front element, its main characteristics are a field of view approaching 180° and severe barrel distortion, the latter producing, in some cases a circular image on the film. This barrel distortion is produced by the extremely wide angle of view of the lens. The circumference of the image circle with a 180° view angle corresponds to a straight line in reality, which means that the only lines reproduced as straight are those passing through the centre of the field of view, and even those tend to be foreshortened towards the edges of the frame.

Early fish-eye lenses had an extremely short focal length – 12mm or less – and a small maximum aperture of around f/8. They did not need a focusing mechanism, therefore, because everything from infinity to near the surface of the front element was in focus. However, designs have progressed and modern fish-eyes are much more advanced. Most now produce an image that completely fills the negative format, and minimum apertures as large as f/2.8 are not unknown; in consequence, focusing mechanisms are now required and most lenses incorporate one. It is not possible to put a filter on the front of a fish-eye lens (it would cause severe cut-off), and provision is made on some lenses to insert filters between the elements. Other lenses have a selection of filters built into the lens, and chosen by turning

a ring on the lens barrel.

The highly distorted images produced by fish-eye lenses would have been considered distinctly undesirable a few years ago (they still are in some circles). But the effect is now used as a creative device by many photographers.

Which wide angle? The choice of a wide angle lens, like that of a telephoto, depends to a large extent on the kind of photography you do. For general purpose work, where you just want to include a little more in your pictures when taking buildings or panoramic views, or where you need extra depth of field, a lens with a focal length of 28mm to 35mm will be suitable. Until quite recently the most popular wide angle lens for a 35mm camera was 35mm focal length, but now the 28–30mm focal length seems to be gaining in favour, probably

because the results are more obviously wide angle. You can also exploit the characteristic of diverging verticals when the lens is pointed down more easily and effectively with a slightly shorter focal length.

If your interest is in photographing architectural interiors, your standard lens will probably be 28mm to 35mm, and for wide angle work you will need something considerably shorter in focal length – perhaps 20mm to

24 The fish-eye lens gives a whole new approach to everyday scenes. This picture of Coventry Cathedral was taken with a 16mm Sigma fish-eye

24mm. If you want to avoid distortion (converging or diverging verticals), be especially careful to keep the camera perfectly level, because these effects are emphasised by shorter focal lengths. When you use ultra wide angle lenses for external architectural pictures without distortion, you have the problem of eliminating unwanted foreground detail. Either you must find an elevated viewpoint or you can make your print from just the top half of the negative. Alternatively you can correct converging verticals when you make the print by tilting the enlarger baseboard.

Contrary to popular opinion, you can use wide angle lenses in portraiture, as long as you do not get too close to your sitter. This means restricting your wide angle portraits to three-quarters or full length, or to taking the subject in the surroundings associated with him – in his office if he is a businessman, for example, or in his greenhouse surrounded by plants if he is a nurseryman. Wide angle lenses give a pleasant informal atmosphere to portraits, and a feeling of spontaneity that is difficult to obtain in any other way.

Despite the fact that wide angle lenses focus down to very short distances, they are not really suitable for close-up work, because of the difficulty of lighting the subject without casting shadows with the lens. The steep perspective given by the combination of short focal length and short camera-to-subject distance does not look very pleasant either.

Because of the extreme distortion you get with fish-eye lenses, you should only use these on very rare occasions. If you use one too often, your pictures will quickly begin to look gimmicky. The high cost of these lenses will probably put them way down on your list of priorities anyway.

Zoom lenses The motion picture and television industries have been responsible for several developments that have found a place in still photography. Among them is the zoom lens, a lens of variable focal length that can be adjusted continually by simply turning or sliding a ring on the lens barrel. The advantages of such an optional system are obvious, especially for colour transparency work, where it allows you to fill the transparency exactly with your subject.

Obviously the main requirement for a zoom lens is that it retains sharp focus as the image size is altered (in other words, as the effective focal length is adjusted). This can be achieved in two ways, by optical compensation and mechanical compensation. The former, which entails moving two or more elements in the lens system – usually the first and third groups in a four-group lens – backwards and forwards simultaneously, is the system most commonly used in zoom lenses for still cameras, mainly because this type of lens is easier, and therefore cheaper, to manufacture. The latter, in which the lens elements are mounted on a cam that enables the separation between the various positive and negative lens elements to be varied, provides superior correction and enables longer zoom ratios to be achieved.

Despite the advantages of zoom lenses, they are not really popular with still photographers for several reasons. Firstly, they are expensive, often costing considerably more than two conventional lenses. Secondly, they are heavy, since they contain a great deal of glass – sometimes fourteen elements or more – and all the zooming mechanism. Finally, however good a zoom lens is, it can never be anything more than a compromise; the results produced are seldom if ever as crisp as those produced by conventional lenses of similar quality.

Zoom ratios vary from some 40–80mm to 200–600mm, so there is plenty of choice if you decide you want one of these lenses. Nikon produce a particularly useful one for their cameras, with a range of 50–300mm; but, as with all zooms, the maximum aperture is rather small at f/4.5.

A set of lenses While the lenses you choose will obviously depend on the kind of photography you are interested in, my own recommendation for general purpose use may be helpful, as it is based on my own outfit. I suggest a 50mm standard lens, a 28mm or 30mm wide angle, a 135mm telephoto, and a 2x teleconverter, which will enable you to convert the 50mm lens into a 100mm for portrait work and the 135mm into a 270mm for sports shots. This basic selection should be perfectly adequate for most of your work, but if you want to add another lens to your collection, I would suggest a 20mm or 23mm wide angle if your interest is in architectural pictures, or a 200mm telephoto if you engage in sports photography.

4 Filters

Filters are some of the most widely used of all photographic accessories. They are also some of the most widely misunderstood. In the early days of photography, filters were essential to correct the spectral sensitivity of the film. The non-colour-sensitive and orthochromatic films in use then were very sensitive to the blue end of the spectrum but totally insensitive to the orange and red end. This meant that blues tended to reproduce very lightly in the print while reds were completely black. The use of a yellow filter reduced the amount of blue light reaching the film, so reducing its effective sensitivity to the blue end of the spectrum and producing somewhat darker tones in the blue areas.

Modern films do not suffer so much from this shortcoming; being panchromatic, they are more or less equally sensitive to light of all colours, and is no longer necessary to use filters for spectral sensitivity correction. Instead, you can use them as creative tools, as one of the controls over your picture.

Whenever you take a monochrome picture, you are transposing a full colour subject into a representation in tones of grey. By using filters you can alter the relation of the greys to each other; filters enable you to modify the light entering your camera through the lens and so control the depth of tone that individual colours in the subject produce in the final print.

Why use filters?

There are several reasons for wanting to use a filter when taking a black and white photograph. In the first place you may want to use a correction filter to alter the tonal values of certain parts of the picture to give natural results. This is somewhat different from using filters to correct major deficiencies in the spectral sensitivity of the film, as with ortho films; it is, in fact, correcting for comparatively minor differences between the spectral sensitivity of the film and that of the human eye.

The eye does not have the same sensitivity to light of all colours. It is at its most sensitive in the middle of the spectrum – to yellow and yellow-green light. At the blue and red ends of the spectrum it is considerably less sensitive, so that it sees yellow, yellow-greens and, to a lesser extent, green and orange, as bright colours compared with reds and blues. Panchromatic film, on the other hand, is more sensitive to blue and blue-green than the eye, but less sensitive to green, yellow and orange, and slightly more sensitive to red. Consequently blues, blue-greens and reds appear lighter in the print than we think they should, while yellows and oranges appear darker. The problem here is relatively simple. We need to make the blues in our picture darker (in a landscape this is the sky, of course) while making the yellows and greens lighter.

Filters, as the name suggests, hold back light of certain colours while allowing free passage to that of other colours. They do not *add* anything to light, they only *remove* something. So the light emerging from the filter has a different composition from that entering it. The colour of the light absorbed by the filter is complementary to the colour of the filter. A yellow filter, for example, transmits red, yellow and green light but absorbs blue light; just how much is absorbed depends on the density of the filter. Orange and red filters also absorb blue light, but considerably more strongly than the yellow. However, these come into the category of contrast filters, dealt with shortly.

As the yellow filter absorbs blue light, the blue areas of the subject will reproduce in the print more darkly than they would without the filter, and yellow objects will reproduce more lightly. The degree of lightening and darkening depends on the depth of the filter: the deeper the colour, the greater the total change.

Another way of using filters is to distort the tonal values of part of the picture to give emphasis to an object. Let us take the sky as an example. An orange or red filter will darken the blue portion of the sky beyond the point where it looks natural and will give the clouds more impact. Again the degree of darkening depends on the density of the filter, and with a red filter you can darken the sky almost to the point of blackness. When filters are used in this way they are called contrast filters.

On the face of it, it seems rather illogical that orange and red filters should darken blue sky more than a yellow, when yellow is the complementary colour to blue. Skylight, however, does not consist solely of blue light, but contains light of all other colours as well, though in much smaller proportions than blue. Since orange and red filters absorb more of the spectrum than does yellow, it follows that the blue of the sky will be absorbed more and will reproduce more darkly in the print.

Contrast filters are particularly useful – essential even – when you are taking pictures of subjects whose colours are those to which the film is equally sensitive. Bluish-greens and orange are typical examples. If you take a picture without a filter of a girl in a dress with a turquoise and orange pattern, the dress will appear as a uniform tone of grey. But if you use an orange filter, the pattern will show good contrast between the light-toned orange areas and the darker turquoise areas. You can get the opposite effect by using a bluish-green filter. Using filters in this way allows you to interpret your subject in any way you like, emphasising some parts and playing down others.

A third type of filter, described later, is the polarising filter. This enables you to take pictures of objects with shiny surfaces, and cut out unwanted reflections from those surfaces. It can also be used to darken the sky in both black and white and colour pictures without altering the tonal or colour values of other objects in the picture.

Filter factors

Since a filter absorbs part of the light entering it, you must increase the exposure to compensate for this lost light. The amount by which you must increase the exposure, the filter factor, depends on the colour and density of the filter, the colour sensitivity of the particular film you are using, the colour tempera-

ture of the light source, and, to a certain extent, on the predominant colour of the subject itself. If the filter factor is 2x, you will need to double the exposure, if it is 3x, you will need to treble it, and so on.

You have, of course, two options open to you for increasing the exposure. You can increase the length of the exposure by moving the shutter speed control to a slower speed, or you can open up the lens to a larger aperture. The particular method you choose will depend on whether you need a fast shutter speed to stop action or a small aperture to give added depth of field. Remember that to double the exposure you must open the lens aperture one stop, to treble it you must open the aperture a stop and a half, and to increase the exposure by four times you open the aperture two stops.

Correct exposure is even more important when you are using filters than when you are not, because incorrect exposure will alter the effect of the filter. Under-exposure increases the effect of the filter, whereas over-exposure reduces it.

The subject itself can have a considerable effect on the filter factor. For example, if the general colouring of the subject is similar to the colour of the filter, and you use the normal factor for this filter, the negative will be over-exposed. Modify the factor to a lower value for this type of shot. Naturally, the opposite problem arises if the subject colours are those which the filter absorbs – those complementary to its own colour. You would then increase the filter factor slightly.

Another influence on the effective filter factor is the colour temperature of the light source. You will notice that different factors are often quoted by the manufacturers for daylight and tungsten light. This is because the colour temperature of daylight is much higher than that of tungsten lighting; in other words, daylight has a much higher blue content than tungsten light. So yellow, orange and red filters need a higher factor in daylight than in artificial light, while blue filters need a lower factor. What the manufacturers do not say, though, is that the factors in their filters vary considerably throughout the day. In the early morning and late evening the colour temperature of daylight is much lower than at midday, because the light is much redder. Consequently the filter factors you normally use for yellow, orange and red filters in daylight will be too high, and they can usually be safely halved. This early morning and late evening light can be made to work for you instead of a filter, since you get practically the same effect at these times without a filter as you do at midday with a yellow filter.

If you have a single lens reflex with TTL

metering, you may be tempted just to screw the filter on the lens and let the meter take care of the necessary exposure increase. Unfortunately it is not quite as easy as that. TTL meters use a cadmium sulphide light-sensitive cell that is much more sensitive to red light than any other colour; its spectral sensitivity is quite different from that of a film emulsion. This means that the exposure the TTL meter tells you is correct for yellow, orange and red filters will, in fact, be too short, and for green and blue filters it will be too long. So all in all you would be better off to establish the correct exposure with the TTL meter before you fit the filter, and then apply the filter factor in the usual way.

Using filters

The best advice I can give you is not to use a filter unless it is absolutely essential. Every filter, no matter how good, is going to degrade the performance of your lens by increasing flare, reducing contrast, and possibly reducing definition. So do not fit a filter on to your camera as a matter of course. Many colour workers leave a UV filter on the camera all the time to act as protection for the lens. Fair enough. But a lens cap will protect it just as well, and that does not degrade the performance of the lens.

Yellow and yellow-green filters Probably the most widely used filter for black and white photography is the pale or medium yellow. Its best known use is to give more natural reproduction of white clouds in a blue sky. (Illus 25). It is equally useful for accentuating the texture of sunlit snow, whose shadows, being lit by skylight, are very blue and normally tend to reproduce too lightly in the print.

For portraits in daylight the yellow filter has its uses, too. It will subdue skin blemishes such as freckles and generally lighten skin tones – rather flatteringly for ladies. If your model has blonde hair, it will lighten that, too.

One of the main reasons for the popularity of the yellow filter is that it absorbs only a small portion of the spectrum and therefore has quite a low factor. Consequently you do not have to increase the exposure too much when using it. Filter factors for yellow filters vary from about 1½x for a pale filter to 4x for a deep one.

Personally, I prefer to over-correct landscape photographs slightly by using a yellow-green filter instead of a straight yellow. This does all that a yellow filter does but also lightens grass and foliage slightly to give better contrast between these areas and the sky. It also helps to increase the detail in different tones of green, and to separate them one from the other. This is particularly useful in spring,

when there are so many different shades of green about.

Daylight factors for yellow-green filters are about 2½x, and in tungsten artificial light about 2x.

Green filters A subtle step on from the yellow-green filter is the pale green, which is useful for studies of leaves in summer; it helps the detail to stand out and accentuates texture. The pale green filter also has a use in indoor portraiture, because it compensates for the strong red content of artificial light by allowing the blue end of the spectrum to pass freely. This means that it also darkens lips, but increases the effect of skin blemishes. Used for outdoor portraits, the pale green filter produces a healthy sun-tanned look, but again freckles and the like can be a problem.

For strong contrast effects a deep green filter will darken reds almost to blackness and lighten greens very strongly. This is useful in flower studies, making red and orange blooms dark and strong, while producing light texture-filled leaves to set them off. Without a filter there would be little difference in tone between the blooms and the leaves.

Filter factors for green filters vary from 2x for pale to 6x for a deep tricolour green in daylight, and about 3x for the pale green in tungsten lighting. The deep green is rather more tricky to use than the pale in artificial light, because it absorbs reds and orange strongly, and therefore removes most of the light emitted by tungsten bulbs. Because of this you will need to carry out tests to find the best factor to use with this filter, or bracket your exposures, taking a factor of 6x as a starting point.

Orange filters Basically the orange filter does everything a yellow filter does, only more so. It absorbs blue light strongly, so that it darkens the sky to a much greater degree, and it improves the texture in woodwork and brick to give greater detail in these objects. One other important use of the orange filter is in the copying of old documents that have become stained over the years; the filter lightens these stains, so that the paper once again appears white and fresh.

An orange filter will cut through haze slightly, so that in this type of weather it is useful for landscape pictures; its effect on hazy days is about the same as that of a medium yellow on a clear day. Haze is made up of

25 (overleaf) A yellow filter's most popular use is to increase the contrast between white clouds and blue sky, as in this picture of Manorbier Castle, taken with a standard lens on 6 × 6cm format
A polarising filter cuts down reflections from glass and other non-metallic surfaces:

minute particles of water, dust, and smoke in suspension in the atmosphere. These particles tend to scatter light falling on them, the degree of scatter depending on the wavelength (or colour) of the light. Blues, violets and greens, which are relatively short wavelengths, are scattered much more than reds and oranges, which have longer wavelengths. Now as an orange filter absorbs light at the blue end of the spectrum, it absorbs the larger part of the scattered light, giving the effect of cutting through the haze.

One important use for an orange filter, which is tied up with this haze-cutting characteristic, is to ensure clear pictures when you are using a fairly long focal length lens. A landscape, for example, taken with a standard lens could be perfectly acceptable, but a picture taken from the same spot with a 300mm lens could show a serious loss of contrast as a direct result of even a small amount of haze in the atmosphere. Fitting an orange filter will remove this possibility. The factor for an orange filter in daylight is roughly 4x and in artificial light about 3x.

Red filters If you want to create really dramatic results in your landscapes, this is the filter to use. The blue sky becomes almost black, and even light summer clouds can be made to look quite stormy. This feature also makes the red filter ideal for use in architectural photography, for in addition to darkening the sky, it lightens the brickwork to throw the buildings into greater contrast and at the same time increases the reproduction of texture in the brickwork.

A red filter can help you to produce really spectacular sunsets. The red, orange and yellow parts of the sunset are reproduced almost white against a dark blue sky and the shadowy areas of the clouds.

The haze-penetration characteristics of the red filter are even more pronounced than those of the orange filter. Haze can be virtually eliminated, making the red filter particularly suitable for long telephoto shots where loss of contrast would otherwise be a serious problem. But be wary of using one for normal landscape work, because all aerial perspective will disappear from the scene, the extreme distance being as clearly defined as the foreground, and the result will be a very flat looking picture.

As they absorb two-thirds of the visible spectrum almost completely, red filters tend to have rather large factors. In daylight 8x is about average, while in tungsten lighting it falls to around 6x.

Pale blue filters While yellow is the most popular colour of filter in general use, pale blue is probably the least popular. Its main use is in artificial light for portraits of men, when it darkens the skin tones to produce a tanned effect, though it does tend to accentuate those skin blemishes again. It also lightens blue eyes slightly, producing more detail in the irises.

The blue filter has several other uses. With haze, for example, it has the exact opposite effect to orange and red filters, emphasising the scattered light, and thereby adding atmosphere to such types of picture as misty morning shots. Another interesting use for a blue filter is in against-the-light pictures taken in daylight. A large proportion of such pictures consists of shadows lit by skylight, which is basically blue, so that a blue filter can often increase the detail in these shadow areas.

The factors for pale blue filters are quite low – $1\frac{1}{2}$x for daylight and 2x for artificial light.

Polarising filters To understand how polarising filters work, you must first know a little about how light travels and behaves. Light is a form of electro-magnetic radiation, rather like radio and sound waves, but vibrating at a much higher frequency. Light rays also vibrate in all directions along the path they take, but when they pass through certain substances, some of these vibrations are absorbed while others are freely transmitted. The light that emerges from such substances is said to be polarised. A similar thing happens when light is reflected from a surface, especially if that surface is transparent.

A polarising filter is made of one of the substances that will polarise the light entering it, and this is what makes it so useful in photography. For instance, if you want to take a photograph of the contents of a shop window but there is a strong reflection from the glass, use a polarising filter. By turning the filter on its axis until the angle of its polarity is at right-angles to that of the polarised light reflected from the window, you can eliminate the reflection without altering the reproduction of the contents of the window.

To understand how this is done, compare a polariser – transmitter or reflector – with an open Venetian blind. When the blind is slightly open, it allows horizontal slits of light to pass through. This light is like that which has been polarised. If you place a second Venetian blind in front of the first, the slits of light will still pass through unhindered, but if you turn this second blind through 90°, all the light will be stopped.

The way in which a polarising filter is used is quite straight-forward for SLR users. You simply fit on the lens, look through the viewfinder and turn the filter until the unwanted

26 Without filter

27 With polarising filter

reflection disappears. Since it is a continuously variable device, no one filter factor can be given. Many polarising filters have various factors engraved on the rim of the mount and you read off the appropriate one when you have set the filter correctly.

Another important use of the polarising filter is to darken skies, but unlike coloured filters it does this without affecting the tonal rendering of other objects in the picture, which means it can be used equally well with colour film as with black and white. It is able to do this because light from the blue sky is polarised, especially that part of the sky at right-angles to the sun.

Polarising filters can be used in combination with ordinary colour filters to give you the effects of both. For example, you can use a yellow filter combined with a polarising filter to darken the sky to a similar degree that you would normally get only with a red filter, but with the other colours in the picture modified by only the amount usual with a yellow filter.

Part 2 Picture Making

5 Subjects for Your SLR

The pictures you will take with your single lens reflex will obviously depend on your individual interests, but a few categories seem to be universal favourites: landscapes, architecture, portraits, candid shots, and close-ups. The latter is dealt with in Chapter 6, since it is much more difficult than the others.

Landscape photography

On the face of it, landscape photography is the simplest form of picture making: the subject is immobile and you can produce acceptable results by merely setting the focus, shutter speed and aperture controls correctly, arranging the view on the focusing screen, and pressing the shutter release. But how often have you done just this and been disappointed with the picture when you have processed and printed it? The reason is that you have failed to capture what it was that made you decide to take the picture in the first place – you have failed to capture the atmosphere. To produce really good landscape photographs you must have a love of the countryside, of the mountains, rivers, lakes, of the whole of nature. Only when you have this love, can you get real feeling into your landscapes. If you look at the work of such great landscape photographers as Ansel Adams and Edward Weston, you will see exactly what I mean.

One of the most important components in a good landscape picture is the sky. Landscapes rarely look right with a plain sky, whether it is plain white or the plain grey given by a clear blue sky. This does not apply so much in colour photography, because you have the colours of the landscape itself to add interest, but in black and white photography you need to choose a day when there is a certain amount of cloud about, and use a yellow, yellow-green, or green filter to increase the contrast between the blue sky and white clouds. If the sky is really dramatic, you can make a picture out of this alone, placing the horizon low in the frame and using an orange filter to give even more contrast.

Scale is tremendously important in landscape pictures; lack of it is probably the cause of more failures than any other single factor. Even the most breathtaking landscape can look disappointingly ordinary on a sheet of bromide paper if there is nothing to tell the viewer how large and distant the mountains are, how deep the valley is, or how high the waterfall. Try to compose your landscapes so that there is some easily recognisable object in the foreground or middle distance to give scale to the whole scene (Illus 28). Trees, a house, an animal, or a human figure are all suitable. In the last case, make sure that the person is suitably dressed and is looking at the landscape; if he is looking at the camera, the picture becomes a photograph of a person with a landscape background, which is exactly what you do not want. Nothing looks more ridiculous than a girl in a summer dress looking as if she has just stepped out of a car (which she probably has), and found herself in the midst of the mountains. What you need is someone in climbing or walking gear, looking as if he belongs in that environment.

Lighting can make or mar any picture, and landscapes are no exception. I have already pointed out the necessity for clouds in the sky, and this automatically gives the best type of lighting, too. The clouds cast shadows

28 (overleaf) An easily recognisable object in the foreground of your picture – such as the boats in this picture of Polperro harbour – helps to give scale

across the landscape, and the direct sunlight gives form to hills and valleys. In landscape photography, as in most other forms of photography, ignore the traditional advice given to amateurs to have the sun behind you when taking your pictures. This will only result in flat lifeless pictures. Instead, have the light coming from well to one side of the camera; this may well entail a wait of perhaps several hours until the sun gets into the right position, but if the picture is worth taking, it is also worth waiting for. One exception, where frontal lighting helps, is when you are using a cloud formation as the main interest in your picture.

Landscapes taken against the light often result in quite spectacular pictures, for this type of lighting tends to simplify the subject into bold masses, eliminating fussy detail and heightening the drama of the whole. You will have to be very careful with your exposure measurement, though, to avoid completely empty shadows or burnt-out highlights. A reduction in development time will help you to retain detail throughout the brightness range. Cut it by about 25 per cent or so.

Dull and overcast days are generally quite unsuitable for black and white landscape work unless, of course, you are trying to depict dullness in the picture – an industrial landscape perhaps. But in colour, dull or even rainy days can transform a landscape into something quite unusual, especially if you choose a colour film that is particularly good for this kind of weather, such as Agfa CT18.

Water in the form of lakes, rivers, canals, or the sea, plays a major part in many landscapes, but needs careful handling if you want to avoid disappointment. If the water is still and reflecting mountains or hills, I like to wait until the sun is slightly in front of the camera, so that I get reflections thrown up from the surface to give a shimmering, sparkling effect to the water. Keep exposure to the minimum to retain subtle tones and highlights in the water. On the sea shore, close shots of rocks with the sea as a background can make interesting pictures, especially if the rocks have limpets or other shellfish stuck to them. You can sometimes increase the tone range in such shots by throwing a bucket of sea water over part of the rocks; this deepens the tone of the rock in parts and may provide a highlight reflection or two.

Waterfalls and rapids need specially careful exposures. If the shutter speed is too slow, the water becomes a blurred mass, which usually looks quite dull, and if it is too fast, it will freeze the motion completely. The ideal answer lies between these two extremes, with the water slightly blurred to give a feeling of movement but sufficiently still so that it does not lose its form. A shutter speed of 1/60 or 1/125 second will normally give you this kind of result.

Mountain photography can be one of the most exciting and interesting forms of landscape photography, but it does present one or two special problems. The first is that ultra-violet radiation is prevalent at high altitudes, so that a yellow or ultra-violet absorbing filter must be used at all times to avoid excessive haze in your pictures. Do not go to anything deeper than yellow, however, because this will remove virtually all the haze and kill any impression of distance. This use of filters is particularly important if you are using a telephoto lens, when the aerial perspective becomes even more noticeable. The telephoto lens is highly suitable for mountain photography as it enables you to shoot pictures that would be unobtainable with shorter lenses, because of inaccessibility.

Advice generally given about lenses for landscape work is to stick with the standard focal length and a mild telephoto, leaving wide angles alone, except for panoramic shots. There is something in this, though a wide angle of about 28mm focal length is ideal for certain types of landscape work – for example, a large object in the foreground – a clump of rocks, reeds at the edge of a lake, or something of the sort – with the rest of the landscape forming a sort of backdrop. In this case the wide angle of view allows me to get the relative scale of the picture components as I want them, and the relatively large depth of field enables me to keep both the foreground object and the distant landscape perfectly sharp. But whichever lens you use, please make sure that you fit it with an efficient lens hood to eliminate any chance of flare, which will reduce the contrast of the image. If you are shooting against the light, hold a map or folded newspaper in front of and above the lens so that it casts a shadow on it; this will increase the efficiency of your lens hood.

The best type of film for landscape work is a slow or medium speed emulsion. If you are carrying a tripod or if the weather is very bright, use the slowest film you can in the interests of fine grain, but a general purpose film such as Ilford FP4 is perfectly adequate for most shots, especially if you do not want to enlarge the negative much more than to 15in by 12in. For pictures in dull or rainy weather, if you are trying to put over these qualities in the shot, use a fast grainy film such as Kodak Tri-X or Ilford HP4, which may often add to the atmosphere by giving texture in the form of inherent grain to otherwise blank areas.

Architecture

It has long been a widespread belief that the only kind of camera suitable for achitectural photography is a technical camera with all the movements necessary to correct distortion, increase depth of field, and so on. While in some cases this is the only type of camera that will give you *perfect* results, for most architectural shots a single lens reflex is quite adequate. Personally, I find the 35mm format ideal, because it forces me to compose the subject as a horizontal or vertical picture.

Buildings, bridges, fountains and other architectural pieces make excellent subjects for the photographer, forming as they do a solid foundation for the effects of light and shade. From just one building you can get a whole range of interesting pictures, and every one will be different. By changing your viewpoint, the angle from which you direct your camera, and the time of day at which you shoot, you can make a building take on all kinds of moods, creating many different impressions.

Apart from pictures of floodlit buildings at night, exterior architectural subjects are always lit by daylight, and in most cases, since buildings rely to some extent on light and shade to reveal their true shape, that daylight will be in the form of direct sunlight. This obviously means that you have no direct control over your light source. You cannot move it or control its intensity, so you have to play the waiting game and go to the site when you know the direction of the light will be right. I have found a very useful addition to my camera bag for just this purpose is a small compass, which I use to determine the orientation of the building, using this information in conjunction with the lighting conditions at the time to decide what time of day approximately will give the best lighting conditions for the picture. The best type of lighting in fact is slightly hazy sunlight, which gives rather luminous shadows, instead of the solid blacks you tend to get with brilliant sunlight and cloudless skies. If you are forced by circumstances to take the shot in contrasty conditions, base your exposure on a shadow reading and cut the development time by a quarter.

Just as important as lighting is perspective; lighting controls the form of the building in the picture, while perspective controls the apparent proportions of the building. Since the standard lens for any camera is designed to produce an image that is more or less as the human eye sees it, pictures tend to look 'natural' if they are taken with this lens. But in many instances a wider angle of view is necessary to include all the building, so a moderate wide angle lens of about 28mm or 35mm focal length is a useful addition to your kit. One

of the biggest problems you are likely to meet in architectural photography – converging verticals – is concerned with perspective. This is the result of tilting the camera upwards to include the full height of a building; there is not a lot you can do about it unless you own a perspective control lens, which has a small amount of vertical or lateral movement – rather like the rising and cross front controls on a technical camera – enabling you to include the top of the building without tilting the camera. If you are really limited for space and are forced to tilt the camera up, do it boldly, so that the convergence of verticals is pronounced. This way it looks as though you meant it, rather than it happened accidentally.

While entire buildings make interesting pictures, you can often make even more attractive ones by concentrating on details – a door and its frame, for example – especially if the building is rather old. If the wood is rough and worn, side lighting will bring out the texture and help to produce a really powerful photograph. When you have photographed a building, therefore, take ten minutes or so to look around for detail shots.

Filters can play an important part in good architectural pictures, particularly medium yellow, orange and red. Of these, the orange is probably the most suitable, because it helps increase the contrast between brickwork and the blue sky, and this makes the building more prominent. It also emphasises clouds and helps to increase the effect of texture in wood. If there are numerous trees in the picture, a green filter may be better, since it will lighten the tone of the foliage while still darkening the sky.

In most cases a slow fine grain film such as Kodak Panatomic-X or Ilford Pan F is best for architectural photography; it records fine detail and subtle textures superbly and the grain is fine enough to enable you to make enlargements up to 20 x 16in with no trouble at all. When using a slow film like this, you will find a tripod essential, for you will often be using a very small aperture and, consequently, a slow shutter speed. If you prefer a somewhat faster film, you can use FP4 or Plus-X; you will not get the same fineness of grain, of course, but it is fine enough for most purposes, and if you are taking architectural interiors, you will find it fast enough to keep time exposures reasonably short.

Most colour films are suitable for architectural work, but try to avoid Ektachrome-X, because of its tendency towards blueness in the shadows. If you are a confirmed Ektachrome user, use it in conjunction with a colour correction filter of about R30.

Achitectural interiors are a little more diffi-

29 This interior shot of Mwnt church near Cardigan was developed by the two-bath technique to control the long tone range. The picture was taken on a 6 × 6cm reflex with standard lens

cult to photograph than exteriors for two reasons. Firstly, since space is usually limited, there are problems in including sufficient to make the picture interesting or meaningful; and secondly, if you are relying on daylight entering the room through visible windows to illuminate the interior, you are faced with extremely long tone ranges (ie the shadow to highlight ratio is large). They are often as large as 500 : 1 or even more.

The only way round the first problem is to use a wide angle lens of 23mm or even 20mm focal length. But you will have to take great care to make sure that the camera is kept perfectly level, for even a very slight tilt will produce quite marked convergence of verticals. You will find a small spirit level a help for this, as you will, of course, be using your camera on a tripod.

The long tone range problem has several solutions. Probably the easiest, but least satisfactory, is to expose and develop your film in the usual way and print it on a very soft grade of paper. A better answer is to increase the exposure slightly (half to one stop) and reduce the development time by about a third. Best of all is to use a two-bath developer (see p 98), which increases separation of tones in the shadow areas while retaining detail in the extreme highlights. The other methods tend to cause a loss of shadow detail.

Portraiture

Just as to make really good landscape photographs you need to enjoy nature, so to make fine portraits you need to like people. You need to understand your subject, be on good terms with him or her, and establish a rapport before you start shooting. If you do not have this sort of relationship, you might just as well leave your camera in its case, because the pictures you get will be stilted, tense and wooden – and what you want is a picture that puts over the personality of your sitter.

The secret of a good portrait is in the lighting, because it is the lighting that accentuates some parts of the face and hides others in shadow. By changing the lighting you can change the whole character of the portrait. The big mistake many photographers make is to use too many lights, with the result that there are crossed shadows cast by the nose and chin (and often on the background by the sitter), and there are multiple catchlights in the eyes. My first piece of advice, therefore, is keep it simple. Personally, I am strictly a one light source man. I believe that the most natural form of lighting for any subject is daylight, so whenever possible I use it; and if I cannot, I use a single lamp, usually covered by a large diffuser. This gives me the closest approximation to daylight that I have yet found.

Sometimes, for male portraits, I use the light source undiffused to give harder results, which emphasise masculinity.

Let us return for a moment to daylight. It is, without doubt, the best lighting of all for nearly every subject – and it is free! It is also the most versatile type of lighting: it can be harsh and bright, casting deep, black shadows; it can be soft and hazy, when the sun is partly obscured by light cloud; or it can be flat, casting extremely soft shadows, when the sun is hidden by thick cloud. Of these, the least suitable is bright harsh sunlight, which causes the sitter to squint through half-closed eyes and wrinkle up his forehead, and gives harsh unflattering shadows. Much better is the softer hazy sunlight that will give modelling to the face without causing screwed-up eyes. Avoid taking portraits when the sun is directly overhead, for it casts ugly shadows in the eyes; it is better to shoot an hour or so before or after noon to get some degree of angle into the lighting. To lighten shadows, if necessary, use such reflectors as a newspaper or aluminium foil, or use a small electronic flash gun. In the latter case be careful how you calculate the flash distance or the results will look false. The correct procedure is first of all to determine the exposure for the highlight side of the face. Then, taking the aperture given by the meter, calculate the distance of the flash from the guide number. The distance given will produce the same intensity of light on the shadow side of the face as that on the sunlit side, and this becomes the starting point. If you want a 2 : 1 highlight-to-shadow ratio, multiply the flash distance by roughly $1\frac{1}{2}$, and if you want a 4 : 1 ratio, double the flash distance. In this way you can fill in the shadows exactly as you want them.

The advantage of reflectors is that the brightness of the light reflected into the shadows can never equal or be greater than the main highlight, so the correct modelling remains, as you originally saw it. If you are taking a portrait with back lighting to give a halo effect to the sitter's hair, use a sheet of white card with a hole in the middle through which you can point the camera lens. This reflector lightens the facial details while retaining the character given by back lighting.

For colour work I prefer cloudy conditions, because the human face seems to photograph better in this weather. I remove any blueness from the light with an R15 or R30 colour temperature correction filter. If you use reflectors with colour film, make sure they are not coloured, or you will find that colour picked up by your sitter's face.

Moving indoors, I still prefer to use daylight whenever possible. I have a large picture window in my study, which makes a perfect light source. Unfortunately it does not face north, so that it has direct sunlight entering it for at least part of the day, but it is quite easy to arrange my photography for the times when the sun is off my window. At these times I get lovely soft side and half top lighting, which is easy to control with one or two large white reflectors. I also use large black card sheets as anti-reflectors to create a definite shadow on one side of the face, by cutting off any reflections from the light-coloured walls of the room.

However desirable the use of daylight indoors may be, there are times when it is just impossible to use it. Maybe you want to take some portraits at night, for example, or the day is so overcast that there is insufficient intensity of light. In these cases you must fall back on artificial light of one sort or another. There seems to be a trend currently away from tungsten lighting towards electronic flash. This is all very desirable, because it removes any possibility of camera shake or subject movement during the very short flash exposure time, but the kind of electronic flash equipment you need for studio work is too expensive for the average amateur budget. True, you can use a small portable electronic flash gun, but if you want to produce soft general lighting, you have to bounce it off a reflector, so that by the time it reaches the sitter it has lost most of its intensity.

Large studio electronic units have adjustable light output to suit the speed of the film, lamp distance, and so on. The correct lamp distance is calculated by simply dividing the flash guide number for the film speed you are using (this figure will be quoted on the flash instruction leaflet) by the aperture at which you want to use the lens. Alternatively, if the distance is set, you can calculate the correct aperture by dividing the guide number by the distance. If you soften the light by bouncing it from a white reflector, use the total distance between the flash head, the reflector, and back to the sitter in your calculation, then open up the lens one stop wider to allow for light absorbed by the reflector. Make sure you have the flash lead plugged into the X socket; in fact if, like me, the only flash you use is electronic, it is a sensible idea to cover the F socket with a piece of adhesive tape, so that you cannot plug in wrongly by mistake.

Tungsten lamps are more economical for the amateur than electronic flash, and can be used in exactly the same way. The only difference is that they need longer exposure times, and will not therefore stop movement with the same efficiency. You can, of course, use a conventional exposure meter to determine the exposure, instead of having to calculate from guide numbers or use a special flash meter. The best type of lighting unit to use – assuming you approve of my soft lighting philosophy – is a very large reflector with a cap that fits over the bulb so that all the light reaching the sitter is reflected; no direct light from the bulb leaves the unit. Alternatively, if you have a small unit, you can reflect the light from a white card in exactly the same way as electronic flash, or use a frame covered with tracing paper or muslin in front of the unit.

Whichever type of artificial lighting you use, you can reduce the highlight-to-shadow ratio by using reflectors, just as you do for daylight. You can also increase the lighting contrast by using black anti-reflectors.

The best lens to use for portraiture is a mild telephoto of 90mm or 100mm. Your 135mm will do at a pinch, but it is rather long, and the camera-to-subject distance will be getting large. At the fairly close distances at which you will be working depth of field tends to be shallow, so to ensure a pleasing result always focus on the model's eyes. This way, even if the rest of the face is going soft, the portrait will appear sharply focused. For full-length portraits a moderate wide angle lens is useful to enable you to record the full height of the subject without having to move back too far. A focal length of 35mm on a 35mm SLR is plenty wide enough; if you go any further than this, you will start to run into trouble with distortion. One of the most useful lenses for portraiture is a 2x teleconverter. Used in conjunction with your standard lens, it gives a combination of 90mm to 110mm, depending on the focal length of the prime lens.

One thing I learned long ago about portraiture was not to be sparing with film. The human face is very mobile, capable of an incredible range of expressions, and only by using lots of film can you hope to capture even a few of these expressions. In addition, especially when your sitter is a stranger, it takes time for him to relax, so the first shots in a session are rarely good ones. Note that I say rarely, not never, so you cannot take a chance and shoot the first dozen pictures with no film in the camera. In a portrait session lasting, say, an hour, I would probably reckon to use at least two and probably three or four 36-exposure cassettes of film.

Backgrounds are a vexatious problem. The traditional way is to use a plain white or black background, and in many cases these are quite suitable; but they do not help to tell you much about your sitter, and a growing practice is to photograph him or her in surroundings that convey something of his or her character. Photograph a craftsman at his workbench, for example, or a book lover in his library. A

30 Whenever possible, I suggest a single light source for portraits. For males a direct light gives strong shadows, which help to emphasise masculinity

31 For softer results with a single light, you can use the light source behind the model to highlight the hair and a reflector in front to lighten the face

useful trick is to arrange the impedimenta of the sitter's profession or hobby on a table in front of him, and use a wide angle lens, so that the items at the front are large enough to be easily recognised. Stop the lens down to give sufficient depth of field to ensure both the foreground and the sitter are sharp.

The best type of film for portraiture is a slow or medium speed one, so that grain does not become a problem. Used in conjunction with an acutance developer for maximum sharpness, this type of film should be suitable for practically all types of portraiture. For colour I cannot think of a better film than Ektachrome-X, which gives superb flesh tones.

Candid pictures

One specialised branch of portraiture, to which none of the information given in the previous section applies, is candid photography – taking pictures of people going about their business without the knowledge that they are being photographed. The acknowledged master of this type of photography is the Frenchman Henri Cartier-Bresson, and I would advise you to study his work to see just what can be done in this field, and what sort of competition you are up against.

The whole purpose of candid photography is to make a comment on society or to tell a story in pictures. You may do this in a single picture or you may take a series, but no matter which form it takes, the candid picture or pictures will record life as it really is.

In many ways the SLR is not the ideal camera for this type of photography; because it is faster to use and generally smaller, the 35mm coupled-rangefinder camera is better. But the SLR comes a very good second, and unless you specialise in candid photography it is hardly worth buying a separate type of camera for the odd occasions when you may use it.

There is very little advice to be given about candid photography, other than to carry your camera at all times, to have it focused on the distance where action is most likely to take place, and to have the shutter speed and aperture controls set to give an exposure that is approximately right. In this way you can shoot first and think afterwards. If you have time to refocus and take an exposure reading, you can always take a second shot which is correctly focused and exposed.

For film I would recommend a high speed emulsion of 400 ASA or so, such as Tri-X or HP4; grain is of little importance in this branch of photography, and with a fast film you can be fairly certain that you have enough versatility to handle subjects in bright light or indoors. Fast film has more latitude than slower film, so that your exposure determination technique need not be as accurate when you are working at speed. Since technique is generally a secondary consideration to the picture itself, it does not matter too much if you have empty shadows or burnt-out highlights. High-speed Ektachrome, or GAF200 and GAF500 are the most suitable colour films.

A telephoto lens of about 135mm focal length is extremely useful for candid photography, since it enables you to observe what is going on as an outsider, as it were. On the other hand, if you want to give the viewer a feeling of being there, try a 28mm wide angle lens and get in among the action.

32 Always be ready for chance shots, such as this tired dealer at the New Forest pony sales, taken with a 135mm lens

6 Close-up Photography

Close-up work is one of the most fascinating aspects of photography, and the single lens reflex is perfect for it – for several reasons. Firstly, the problem of parallax, which can be most troublesome in other camera types, does not arise, because you view the subject through the taking lens and you take exactly what you see. Secondly, focusing is greatly simplified. Close-up pictures depend on pin-sharp definition of the fine detail, so that accurate focusing is absolutely essential. With the SLR there is no need for tape measures, or other measuring devices, and by using the preview button on the lens, you can see exactly what depth of field you will have at the stop you want to use. Finally, if your SLR has through-the-lens metering, automatic account is taken of any accessories you place in front of the lens or between the lens and the camera body. This is a big advantage, for exposure problems in close-up photography can be quite complicated, and without TTL metering a great deal of mathematics or referring to tables is necessary.

The closest distance at which a normal lens on an SLR will focus is 12–18in, so, to take pictures at any distance less than this, you must fit some sort of device to the camera to increase the distance between the lens and the film plane. You can do this physically by means of extension tubes or bellows, or effectively by placing a supplementary lens in front of the camera lens.

In this chapter several optical formulas will be used. Before going any further, therefore, here are the symbols and abbreviations I shall be using throughout:

f = focal length
u = lens-object distance
v = lens-image distance
D = object-image distance
M = linear magnification
R = linear reduction
e = length of extension tubes or bellows

Supplementary lenses

The simplest and least expensive way of taking close-ups is to fit a supplementary lens – often called a close-up lens – on to the front of the camera lens. Just because the close-up lens is cheap and simple, do not despise it, for it has certain advantages over the more sophisticated extension tubes and bellows.

Of course, if your camera does not have interchangeable lenses, the supplementary lens offers the only possible means of taking close-up pictures, because there is no way of physically increasing the lens-image distance. However, when you fit a supplementary close-up lens, you decrease the focal length of the camera lens; so in effect you have increased the lens-image distance. An example will make this clear.

If you have a camera with a 50mm focal length lens and fit a supplementary lens of 500mm focal length to it, the effective focal length of the combination will be:

$$f = \frac{f_1 \times f_2}{f_1 + f_2}$$

where f = effective focal length of the combination
f_1 = focal length of the camera lens
f_2 = focal length of supplementary lens

$$\therefore f = \frac{50 \times 500}{50 + 500} = 45.45mm$$

But since the camera lens is still fixed at a distance of 50mm from the film plane, you now have a lens of 45.45mm focal length at 50mm from the film – an effective extension of 4.55mm. The combination of camera lens and supplementary lens will focus at:

$$u = \frac{v - f}{v \times f} = \frac{50 \times 45.45}{50 - 45.45} = 500mm$$

The focusing distance is, as you will no doubt have noticed, exactly the same as the focal length of the supplementary lens. This fact always applies, no matter what the focal length of the camera lens. But this focusing distance only holds good when the camera lens is focused at infinity. When it is set at a distance less than infinity (ie when the lens-film distance is increased), the combination will enable you to focus on objects at distances closer than the focal length of the supplementary lens. The formula above still applies, but now that the lens-image distance, v, has been increased you must determine the new value of v first. Assuming the camera lens is set to 1m (1,000mm or approximately 39in):

$$v = \frac{u \times f}{u - f} = \frac{1,000 \times 50}{1,000 - 50}$$
$$= 52.63mm$$

The new object distance will be:

$$u = \frac{v \times f}{v - f} = \frac{52.64 \times 45.45}{52.64 - 45.45}$$
$$= 331mm$$
(approximately 13in)

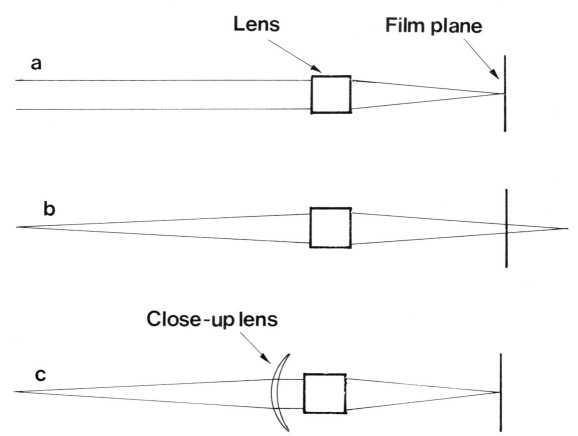

Lens   Film plane

a

b

Close-up lens

c

33 How a close-up lens works:
(a) Light from an object at infinite distance is in parallel rays and comes to a focus at the film plane
(b) Light from an object at a very short distance from the lens is not in parallel rays, and the lens focuses it at some point behind the film plane
(c) Adding a positive supplementary lens with a focal length the same as the subject distance modifies the light rays, so that they are parallel when they enter the camera lens and again become focused at the film plane

Supplementary close-up lenses are given dioptre numbers rather than focal lengths for the purpose of identifying them, but it is a simple matter to convert the dioptre number into a focal length for making your calculations. The dioptre is simply the reciprocal of the focal length of the lens in metres. So a +1 dioptre supplementary lens has a focal length of 1m, a +2 has one of 500mm, and a +3 one of 333mm. The plus sign merely indicates that the lens is positive or magnifying.

Fortunately you do not have to work out all these calculations every time you want to take a close-up picture with an SLR. You just screw the supplementary lens on the camera lens and focus in the usual way. But it is as well to understand the formulas so that you can follow the theory behind the supplementary lens. A full table of subject distances at various focus settings for a range of close-up lenses is given in Appendix 5 (p 122).

One of the most useful properties of supplementary close-up lenses is that they are additive, ie you can use two or more together to make the equivalent of a single lens of the total power of the individual lenses. For example, you can use a +1 and a +3 to give the same effect as a +4. This enables you to take pictures at quite close range even if your camera is a non-interchangeable lens model. But it is best to keep the number of individual lenses to the minimum, because every extra element you introduce between the subject and the film increases the risk of flare and loss of contrast. The cause of this is the large number of glass-to-air surfaces. For this reason it is also important to use coated supplementary lenses whenever possible.

One criticism often levelled at close-up lenses is that you get falling off of definition if you use them with the camera lens set at a wide aperture. This is quite true, but when you are taking close-up pictures, the depth of field produced is very small, and in order to increase it, you need to stop the lens down to at least f/8. By this time only the centre of the supplementary lens is being used, and the definition produced is perfectly adequate.

Scale of reproduction To reproduce an image of an object on your negative the same size as the object itself would need a supplementary lens with the same focal length as your camera lens. With a 50mm lens, therefore, you would need a +20 dioptre supplementary. Single meniscus lenses of the type normally used for supplementaries are quite impracticable to produce at anything even approaching this power – in fact it is rather tricky to produce a successful meniscus lens of a power higher than +10 – so that when you take close-up pictures using supplemen-

tary lenses, the image on the negative will always be smaller than the object itself.

There is a way round the problem, however. Adapter rings, which are now available, enable you to use one of your camera lenses on the front of another. In this way your standard 50mm lens becomes a high quality 20 dioptre supplementary lens. If you have two 50mm lenses, you can therefore take subjects at life size, or you can use one in conjunction with a telephoto lens – say 135mm – to get reproduction ratios of about 3 : 1.

The formula for calculating the scale of reproduction for a close-up is:

$$R = \frac{u - f}{f}$$

So taking the combination of 50mm camera lens and 500mm (+2 dioptre) supplementary as before, and with the camera lens at infinity,

$$R = \frac{500 - 45.45}{45.45} = 10 : 1$$

What this means is that an object 5in high would produce an image $\frac{1}{2}$in high on the negative. In other words, the object area that will fill the whole of a 35mm negative is 15 x 10in.

The advantages of supplementaries Despite the fact that supplementary lenses are simple and inexpensive, they have a number of advantages over such other methods of taking close-up pictures as extension tubes and bellows. Firstly, close-up lenses need no increase in exposure, because the lens-image distance remains unaltered no matter what power the supplementary is. On the other hand, when you use either extension tubes or bellows, the lens-film distance is increased and the aperture numbers marked on the lens barrel no longer apply. Instead, the effective aperture is reduced quite considerably – as much as five or six stops if you are using a really long extension with a short focal length lens. Secondly, supplementary lenses are small. You can carry a whole range of them in your wallet with no trouble, as long as they are adequately protected, of course.

Finally, as I explained earlier in this chapter, supplementary lenses are additive. If you buy one each of 1, 2, 3, and 4 dioptre, you will theoretically be able to use them in combination to give you powers up to 10 dioptre. But try not to use more than two lenses together except in emergencies, to avoid the danger of flare.

Getting the best from supplementaries Always use your supplementary lenses as close as possible to the front element of your camera lens to minimise the effects of adding two more glass-to-air surfaces to the system. In this way the supplementary becomes almost an integral part of the camera lens. If you want to use a filter as well as a supplementary, always place the filter on last, so that the distance between the supplementary and the camera lens is not increased.

Whenever possible, use the camera lens at a stop smaller than f/8 to provide adequate depth of field and minimise the effects of aberrations which are inevitably introduced by the supplementary. The most troublesome of these is chromatic aberration, which causes light of different colours to come to a focus at different points or planes, giving the well known rainbow effect, especially around white objects on colour transparencies. Although the effect is not so noticeable in black and white pictures, it is there nevertheless. If you stop the lens down to increase the depth of field of the subject, it also increases the depth of focus at the image plane. This means that light of all colours will be within the depth of focus and will appear to come to a focus at the same point.

Extension tubes and bellows

If you want to take life-size or larger pictures of your subjects, and your camera has interchangeable lenses, the easiest and most successful way is to use extension tubes or bellows. In some ways extension tubes are rather similar to supplementary lenses, in that they give you a fixed reproduction ratio, but unlike supplementaries they do not take the edge off the optical performance of the camera lens by introducing aberration effects. Extension tubes are usually sold in sets of three or four, which can be used individually or in any one of a number of different combinations. A typical set may have lengths of 6, 14, 30 and 45mm, giving fifteen combinations of extension length for reproduction ratios from 0.12 : 1 up to 1.9 : 1 – nearly twice life size. Several sets are now available with a through coupling to enable the automatic aperture of the camera lens to continue working even at extreme close-up range. An alternative arrangement is a special extension tube with a built-in mechanism operated by a cable release to activate the automatic aperture.

Extension bellows are, in effect, continuously variable extension tubes. They are considerably more expensive than tubes, but they are also considerably more versatile, so the extra money is well spent. The main drawback of extension bellows is their lack of rigidity. Because there is, of necessity, a flexible coupling between the lens and the camera body, they are not quite so resistant to vibration, but if you take great care to avoid touching your tripod immediately before you press the shutter release, you should not be troubled unduly by camera – or bellows unit – shake.

Reproduction ratios

The ratio of the size of the object you are photographing to the size of the image of that object formed at the film plane in your camera is called the reproduction ratio, and can be a magnification, M, or reduction, R. It is also the ratio of the lens-object distance, u, to lens-image distance, v. This can be written mathematically as:

$$M = \frac{v}{u}$$

To establish the reproduction ratios for various extension lengths would call for a great deal of measuring, but fortunately there is a way of short-cutting this procedure:

$$u = \frac{v \times f}{v - f}$$

and if you substitute this for u in the original formula, you get:

$$M = \frac{v - f}{f}$$

In this case v will be equal to the focal length of your camera lens plus the extension length you are using:

$$v = f + e$$

So you can simplify the formula still further to:

$$M = \frac{e}{f}$$

Here is an example so that you can see just how simple it all is. Suppose you are using a 50mm camera lens and a combination of extension tubes, making a total length of 80mm:

$$M = \frac{e}{f} = \frac{80}{50} = 1.6 : 1$$

If the length of the extension tubes or bellows is less than the focal length of the camera lens, the image on the negative will be smaller than the original object, so the reproduction ratio will be a reduction. This means that you must turn the formula upside down to retain a ratio larger than 1:

$$R = \frac{f}{e}$$

For example, if you are using a 90mm lens on a 40mm extension, the reproduction ratio will be:

$$R = \frac{f}{e} = \frac{90}{40} = 1 : 2.25$$

The reproduction ratios for various combinations of extension length and focal length of lens are given in Appendix 5 (p 000). From the table there and from the formulas above you will see clearly that the extension length for any particular reproduction ratio depends entirely on the focal length of the lens you are using. The longer the focal length of the lens, the longer must the extension be for a given reproduction ratio. On the face of it, then, it would perhaps appear that the best lens to choose for close-up work on tubes or bellows would be one of short focal length, since a lens of this type would enable you to cover a wider range of reproduction ratios.

Exposure correction

When you use extension tubes or bellows for close-up photography, your exposures are complicated by the fact that the effective aperture of the camera lens changes as you change the extension length. Aperture is indicated by the f/numbers marked on the lens barrel, which are the ratios of the focal length of the lens to the diameter of the aperture through which the light passes at the various settings. For example, a 100mm lens with the iris diaphragm set at a diameter of 9mm would have an f/number of 100/9, which is roughly equal to f/11 for that setting. If the iris diaphragm is opened up to a diameter of 18mm, the f/number would be 100/18 or approximately f/5.6. But these f/numbers only hold true when the lens is at or near a distance equal to its focal length from the film plane. As the lens-image distance is increased, the effective aperture becomes smaller, the actual value being determined by this formula:

$$a = \frac{b \times v}{f}$$

where
a = effective f/number
b = marked f/number
v = $e + f$

So if you are using a lens of 50mm focal length set at f/8 and an extension length of 100mm, the effective aperture will be:

$$a = \frac{b \times v}{f} = \frac{8 \times 150}{50} = f/24$$

Using this formula you would have to calculate the effective aperture every time you wanted to take a picture, or spend a lot of time making up tables of effective apertures at various extension lengths. However, there is an easier way; you can work out an exposure correction factor, X, which can then be applied to any f/number you like:

$$X = \frac{(e + f)^2}{f^2} \text{ or } (M + 1)^2$$

If we take as an example the 50mm lens and 100mm extension again, giving a reproduction ratio of 2 : 1,

$$X = (2 + 1)^2 = 3^2 = 9$$

Now as each stop increase gives an exposure increase factor of two, an increase of nine

times means that the lens must be opened by three and a third stops from the indicated aperture to retain the effective aperture. An indicated aperture of f/22 would need an actual aperture setting of f/7.

From all this you will see that the exposure increase is dependent entirely on the reproduction ratio and not on the physical length of the extension tubes or bellows. Appendix 5 gives exposure correction factors and exposure increases for a variety of reproduction ratios.

Of course, if your SLR is fitted with through-the-lens matering, all these exposure problems will be solved automatically when you take a meter reading. If you intend to use your camera extensively for close-up photography with extension tubes or bellows, it is certainly worth spending a little extra to buy a model with TTL metering for this very reason.

Reciprocity failure

If you are taking a close-up at a reproduction ratio of, for example, 5 : 1, you will have to increase the exposure time by thirty-six or open the lens aperture by just five stops. Owing to the limited depth of field possible in close-up pictures, you will be more likely to take the first course of action, and this will almost certainly mean that the exposure time will be more than 1 second. This will bring you into contact with a phenomenon called reciprocity failure.

Bunsen and Roscoe discovered in the 1850s that a piece of film exposed to light for a certain length of time responded in exactly the same way as a second piece of film exposed for twice the length of time to a light half as strong. They called this their Reciprocity Law. In modern photographic practice, it says, in effect, that a piece of film exposed for 1/125 second at f/8 will produce a negative, when developed, which looks identical with one exposed for 1/60 second at f/11. Applying this law a little further, it would be reasonable to expect a piece of film exposed for 4 seconds at f/16 to look the same as one exposed for $\frac{1}{2}$ second at f/5.6; but in fact the Reciprocity Law fails when exposures of longer than 1 second are given, and you have to apply a correction factor. Instead of a 4 second exposure at f/16, you would have to allow 6 seconds at f/16 to produce a negative identical with that exposed for $\frac{1}{2}$ second at f/5.6. The Reciprocity Law also fails at very short exposures – shorter than about 1/1,000 second – and if you use a high speed electronic flash gun, you will have to take this into account, especially when you use colour transparency film.

An added difficulty is that negative films and reversal films need different correction factors,

although both monochrome and colour films are covered by these factors. Full tables of reciprocity failure corrections are given in Appendix 4 (p 122).

If you have a single lens reflex without TTL metering, the full procedure for determining the correct exposure for a close-up picture is as follows:

1 Take an exposure meter reading either direct from the subject or, if the subject is very small or inaccessible, from a piece of grey card.
2 Apply the correction factor for the reproduction ratio at which you are taking the picture.
3 To the corrected exposure time apply the correction factor for reciprocity failure.

You must always carry out the procedure in this order. Here is an example.

Assume that you are taking a close-up at a reproduction ratio of 3 : 1, using reversal colour film. The meter reading indicates that you need to give an exposure of 1 second at f/16. Look up the correction factor for the reproduction ratio – in this case – and multiply

34 A gipsy hawk moth taken with a 135mm lens on extension bellows. It was lit by a small desk lamp

35 These Michaelmas daisies are typical of the close-ups that can be taken without special equipment if your lens focuses to a close distance such as 1ft.

the exposure by this factor. You will almost certainly need the small aperture to give adequate depth of field, so the corrected exposure will be 16 seconds at f/16. Now you must correct this exposure for reciprocity failure, and this gives you a final exposure of 32 seconds at f/16. That is a big difference from the original exposure indicated by the exposure meter.

The main thing to remember is always to correct for the reproduction ratio first and then for reciprocity failure. If you do it the other way round, you will not get the right exposure. In the example we have just looked at the exposure would be only 16 seconds instead of the correct 32.

Telephoto converter

The telephoto converter is an accessory not usually associated with close-up work. It is a three- or four-element corrected negative lens that screws on to the back of any lens to increase its effective focal length by two, three, or even four times. But because it does this by modifying the light beam after it has left the basic lens, it does not affect the focusing scale – and therefore the minimum focusing distance – of the camera. This means, of course, that you can focus your lens to, say, 18in, and with a 3x converter fitted, get an image the same size as that produced by the basic lens focused at 6in.

Using a 50mm basic lens that focuses to about 12in with a 2x telephoto converter gives you an extremely useful combination, equivalent to a 100mm macro lens. It provides continuous focusing from infinity right down to approximately same-size reproduction (1 : 1).

Naturally you cannot have all these advantages for nothing; there are disadvantages as well. You need to increase the indicated aperture by two stops when using a 2x converter – an indicated f/8 becomes an effective f/16 – or three stops when using a 3x converter. Alternatively you can increase the exposure time by two or three times to compensate.

Helpful accessories

If you intend to do a great deal of close-up photography, there are one or two accessories that can make life easier for you. The first is a focusing slide. When you are working at close range, you often need to change the camera distance from the subject slightly to compose the picture or fill the frame with your subject. A focusing slide helps you to do this precisely, for it is, in essence, a camera mount running on rails, rather like the focusing mechanism on extension bellows.

Camera lenses give their best performance at distances between 3ft or so and infinity, when the lens-to-subject distance is much greater than the lens-to-film distance. But when you are working at reproduction ratios greater than 1 : 1, the lens-to-film distance is greater and the lens performance tends to suffer. The obvious thing to do in a case like this – or for any close-up using a reasonable extension on the lens – is to turn the lens round so that the rear element is facing forward. Many manufacturers now make a special reversing ring to enable you to do this.

If you are using your camera near ground level, you will often find it difficult to look into the viewfinder. A right-angle finder, which you can attach to the normal eyepiece of the camera, solves this problem completely. It is also useful if the camera is looking straight down on top of a subject. There are a few SLRs – notably the Nikon – which have interchangeable viewing systems; and with these cameras you can replace the pentaprism with a so-called waist-level finder, which eliminates the need for a right-angle finder attachment.

Finally, a focusing magnifier that enlarges the centre portion of the focusing screen is extremely useful. As depth of field at close distances is very small, focusing accurately can be difficult, and the magnified image eases the problem considerably.

Lighting for close-ups

Although clear bright sunlight is ideal for lighting close-ups – it produces sharp clean shadows – daylight in general is not really suitable, for you have no direct control over it. In addition, the quality and brightness of daylight is almost continuously changing, which can make exposure determination rather difficult.

Another disadvantage is that, when you are taking close-ups at reproduction ratios greater than 1 : 1, daylight is just not bright enough, unless you are using direct sunlight. While this may seem difficult to believe at first sight, remember that you have to increase the exposure indicated by your meter when you use a long extension, and you are more or less obliged to use a small aperture to get the necessary depth of field. In consequence, exposure time is likely to be in the order of seconds rather than fractions of a second, especially if you are using a relatively slow colour reversal film; and if there is the slightest breeze, or if the subject is rather lively, your pictures will be blurred.

One way in which you can solve the problem of wind causing subject movement is to surround the subject on three sides with a sheet of thin clear acetate, which you can buy from any commercial artists' supplier. Fix it with clothes pegs to two 3ft lengths of garden cane pushed into the ground on either side of the subject and slightly in front of it. This method shields the subject from breezes, but does not cast shadows or interfere with the background.

If you have to use daylight, you can increase the level of illumination by means of reflectors. Small handbag mirrors are good for this job, but perhaps the small concave mirrors sold as shaving mirrors are even better. Used carefully, these concave mirrors enable you to concentrate quite a large amount of light on the subject – rather like a small spotlight. But if you have a delicate subject be careful not to place it at the focal point of the mirror; a concave mirror acts in exactly the same way as a magnifying lens, giving the same burning-glass effect at its focal point.

Fill-in lighting is best provided by small reflectors made from white card or from card covered with kitchen foil. Both these reflectors and the handbag mirrors can be supported by bulldog clips or simple stands made from stiff wire.

Tungsten lighting Because you can control it

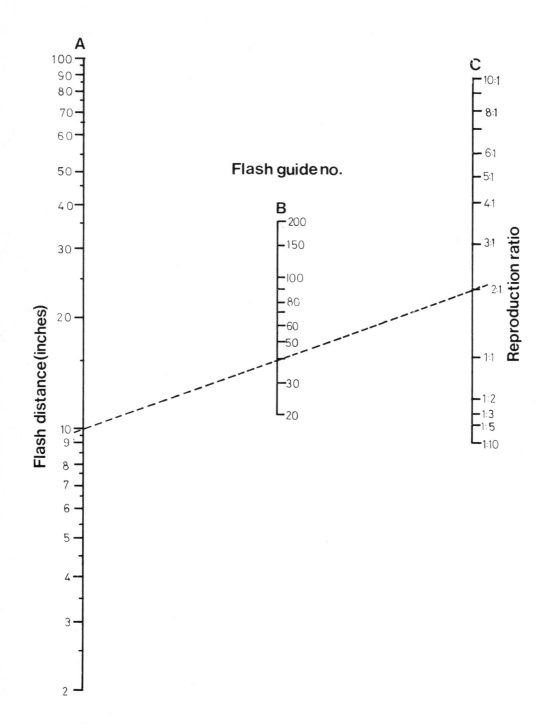

A

Flash distance (inches)

100
90
80
70
60
50
40
30
20
10
9
8
7
6
5
4
3
2

Flash guide no.

B

200
150
100
80
60
50
30
20

C

Reproduction ratio

10:1
8:1
6:1
5:1
4:1
3:1
2:1
1:1
1:2
1:3
1:5
1:10

36 Chart for calculating flash distance at f/16. Lay a straightedge through the normal guide number of the flash on scale B and reproduction ratio on scale C. Read off the flash distance on scale A

to give exactly the effect you want, tungsten lighting is far more suitable for close-up photography than daylight. Its only real disadvantage is the amount of heat generated. Fortunately, though, high-powered lamps are not necessary, because you can use lights at only a few inches from the subject and keep the exposure times quite short. Lamps of about 100W are generally adequate for most close-ups.

The reflectors that are usually sold as photographic floodlights are not suitable for most close-up work, since they spread the light over too wide an area. As the subject is very small, this type of reflector bathes everything in light of more or less equal brightness, and the resulting picture tends to look very flat. This applies only to black and white work, where you depend on tonal contrasts for interest; in colour close-ups you have the contrasts provided by the different colours in the subject. In fact, for colour work, soft even lighting is usually an advantage, because it does not cast deep black shadows that tend to mask colour contrasts.

However, to get back to black and white work for a moment, you can easily modify your photoflood reflectors by fitting long tapered tubes of white card to them to cut down the effective area of the light source and make the illumination more directional. These tubes – or snoots as they are called in professional studios – should have an opening of about 3in at the front.

Some of the small modern desk lamps might almost have been made for lighting close-ups. I have two: one is in the form of a cylinder about 8in long and of 3in diameter, and takes bulbs up to 75W; and the other is somewhat smaller in diameter and takes bulbs up to 60W. Both are ideal for close-up work.

Although you can use as many lamps as you like to light your close-ups, I have found that more than one is seldom necessary or even desirable. As I have explained elsewhere in this book, I am strictly a one light source photographer whenever possible, because I find that the results are much more natural that way. If I want to lighten part of the subject, I use reflectors of white card or foil. A particularly useful reflector is one with a hole in it that fits around the camera lens. You can then light your subject from the side or back to bring out the texture, and the reflector just throws enough light back into the shadows to prevent them blocking up completely.

Flash In my opinion the best type of lighting for close-ups by far is electronic flash. It gives a very bright, extremely short flash of light that is sufficient to freeze even the liveliest subjects, yet it still allows you to use a small aperture for maximum depth of field. Unlike tungsten lighting, flash does not generate constant heat, so you can use it at very close quarters without fear of harming the most delicate subject. It has one disadvantage, though: you cannot see the effect of changing the position of the lamps instantly, but have to wait until you have developed the film. The latest studio flash units, however, have overcome this problem by building in a small tungsten modelling light for setting up the subject. This can be switched off when the exposure is made.

By far the biggest problem in using flash for close-ups is that old question of exposure determination. The guide numbers quoted for the flash unit no longer apply when you are using extension tubes or bellows, since the increased extension reduces the effective aperture of the lens, as I explained earlier. Normally you can calculate the correct aperture to use by dividing the guide number by the flash-to-subject distance. But when you use flash for close-ups, you have to modify the calculation to take the reproduction ratio into consideration:

$$a = \frac{GN}{d (M + 1)}$$

where a = aperture
d = flash-to-subject distance
GN = guide number for normal use

For example, if you are using a flash unit with a guide number of 50 at a distance of 2 ft to light a subject you want to reproduce at twice

$$a = \frac{50}{2 (2 + 1)} = \frac{50}{6} = 8.34$$
$$= f/8 \text{ approx}$$

This is a rather tedious procedure to go through every time you take a shot, so I have worked out a chart in Illus 36 that will give you the correct flash distance instantly. To use it, simply place a straightedge so that it passes through both the guide number on scale B and the reproduction ratio on scale C, then read off the correct flash distance on scale A. The chart is designed for an aperture of f/16, since this is perhaps the most useful aperture for close-up work. You can, of course, use the chart at apertures other than f/16, but the flash distances have to be modified. For example, if you use an aperture of f/8, all the flash distances must be doubled, and at f/32, they must be halved.

37 Framing part of the subject with an arch or bridge is an effective way of concentrating interest. Coventry Canal Basin, taken with a 30mm Lydith lens.

7 Composition

Photography, like any other art form, is a combination of two quite different factors: technique and artistic interpretation. You need to master both these factors if you want your photographs to mean something to the person who is looking at them.

Most of this book is directed towards the technique of photography, because this is something that can be taught and mastered relatively simply; it is specific or objective. The artistic side of photography is much more difficult to teach, since it is intangible and subjective; it depends entirely on how you react to your subject and decide to interpret it. You have to decide on the viewpoint from which you take the picture, the focal length of the lens you use, the arrangement of the subject components within the negative or transparency, and many other factors – and they are all highly personal decisions. Only *you* can decide because only *you* know what you want the picture to say. All I can do in this chapter is give you an introduction to the principles of composition in the hope that this will put you on the right road to taking better pictures.

Isolate your subject

When I was studying photography at my local College of Art, one of the things my tutor was always stressing was, 'It's not what you put in your picture that counts, it's what you leave out'. This is good advice, because the beginner always has the tendency to get too much into his pictures, with the result that everything looks jumbled together and confused. So the first thing you must do is select what goes into your picture. Never include more than is absolutely essential; simplicity is the essence of a good picture.

As an exercise to carry out on a dark winter evening, try reappraising some of your existing photographs to see how they could be improved by cutting out some of the unnecessary elements. To help you with this, make a pair of L-shaped pieces of card with arms about 8 or 10in long and an inch or so wide. Place these cards on your print so that the two Ls form a rectangle enclosing part of the picture, then move them about, altering the shape and size of the rectangle while studying the picture within the rectangle. You will be surprised how often you can make perhaps as many as half a dozen different pictures from a single print in this way. Mark all the different pictures on the print, and, next time you have a printing session, make some full-size enlargements from them. In this way you will soon learn to be on the lookout for unnecessary objects in your pictures, and how to make several quite different pictures from a single subject.

While it is quite acceptable to make your picture at the printing stage in this way, it is always far better if you can learn to carry out the selection and composition processes before you press the shutter release to take the picture. The reason is that you are more likely to get a really good picture if you fill the negative frame with the subject as you want the final print to appear. The amount of control you have over the picture at the printing stage is also comparatively small. For example, you cannot change the relation of the foreground to the background when you are making the print. When you compose your picture at the taking stage, you may change your viewpoint very slightly and this can make the difference between a good picture and a superb one – it is impossible

78

to do this at the printing stage. In addition, you start out with a bigger image on your negative, so that you do not have to enlarge so much, and this helps print quality a lot.

When you have decided what you want in your picture, you must next select a suitable viewpoint, so that all the elements are arranged pleasantly within the frame. This is the real art of composition.

Picture format

Composition, really, is applied common sense – arranging your picture to suit the subject you are photographing. For example, if the subject is a landscape with a line of tall poplar trees large in the foreground, avoid using a horizontal format. If you do, either you will not get the full height of the trees in or there will be so little space above and below them that they will appear squashed and out of proportion. If you use a vertical format, the height of the trees will appear to be increased, and they will look more dynamic because they have more space above and below them.

This question of format or picture shape is one of the most important factors in composition, as it determines the whole mood of the picture. A vertical proportion, as we have just seen, gives the picture a dynamic thrusting character, emphasising height and visual depth, whereas a horizontal format gives a feeling of restfulness and expanse. Between the two is the square, which gives a down to earth, stable quality to pictures. In fact it can often produce dull pictures if you are not careful.

Depth

Always remember that you are trying to depict a three-dimensional subject on a two-dimensional piece of paper. This means that you have to introduce a feeling of depth. This can be done in several ways, of which perspective is one.

There are two quite distinct kinds of perspective – geometric and aerial. Geometric perspective governs the relative sizes of the objects in the picture, and depends on the camera-to-subject distance. The nearer you are to an object, the larger it appears; so if you are looking at a photograph of, say, a street, the houses in the foreground will look very much bigger than those in the background. Yet your brain knows that all the houses are more or less the same size and tells you that here, in fact, is a two-dimensional representation of a three-dimensional subject.

Aerial perspective is the well known effect caused by haze in the distance in landscape shots. For example, distant mountains appear to be of a lighter tone than closer objects, and this adds depth to your picture. Interesting

use can be made of aerial perspective in conjunction with a long focal length lens. Since the lens enlarges the size of the subject within the negative frame, it apparently flattens geometric perspective, so that objects at increasing distances from the camera appear to be close together. But aerial perspective causes them to be increasingly lighter in tone the further away they are.

Another way in which you can introduce a feeling of depth into your pictures is to have a large object, preferably in shadow, in the immediate foreground. An obvious, if rather overplayed, way of doing this is to take the picture through an archway or bridge (Illus 37).

The focal point

One of the most important decisions you must make when composing your picture is which part of the subject is to pre-dominate. You need to make it the most eye-catching component of the picture without, generally, making it too obvious. There are several ways in which you can do this – by tone, by size, and by sharpness. If the main subject of your picture is much lighter or much darker than the rest of the picture, it will tend to attract the viewer's eye more easily. Where there are several objects in the picture all of similar brightness, a little burning in at the printing stage will often help. Generally speaking, the larger an object is within the picture, the more important it becomes. So to make sure that the person who looks at your picture sees the same main object as you want him to, try to make it bigger by getting closer to it or by using a lens of longer focal length. Alternatively, try using a wide angle lens, so that you can get really close to the main object and make it very large, allowing the exaggerated perspective given by the close viewpoint to make the background small and relatively insignificant. Sharpness is one your most important and easy-to-use tools. If you really want to concentrate the viewer's attention on a particular object, focus on it, and use a large aperture to throw everything else out of focus. That cannot fail.

Arranging the picture

We now come to perhaps the most important part of the whole composition process – positioning the elements within the negative or transparency frame. My own feeling is that if it looks right, it is right, but there is one way in which you can virtually guarantee a pleasant picture every time. That is by using what is known as the Golden Mean (Illus 38), a way of dividing up space in a certain ratio, which has been used by artists and architects since classical Greek times. The Golden Mean can

38 Horizontal lines and composition give a quiet, peaceful character to a picture. These boats moored in the Lymington River, Hampshire, were photographed with a 50mm Tessar

39 The most dynamic lines in a picture are diagonals because they suggest action. Taken at Southbourne with a 135mm lens

$$A+B:B=B:A$$

40 The Golden Mean. This can be used in several ways to ensure pleasant picture arrangements
The way you hold your exposure meter governs the results you get:

be expressed mathematically as follows: if a line is divided into two unequal parts, the ratio between the complete line and the larger division should be equal to the ratio between the larger division and the smaller division. In practical terms this works out to a ratio of 5 : 8, which, although it is not exactly in conformity with the mathematical definition, is near enough visually.

You can use the Golden Mean in several ways in your photography. Firstly, you can use it for the proportions of your picture; a format with the ratio 5 : 8 or 8 : 5 will give pleasing results, and if you use 35mm, you will find that the picture size is already very close to this ratio. Secondly, you can use it to position the horizon in a landscape, either with the smaller part at the top or the bottom, depending on the rest of the subject. Then you can use the Golden Mean to divide a composition into satisfying proportions by placing the main object on the Golden Mean either horizontally or vertically. Finally, you can create a focal point by placing an object at the point where the vertical and horizontal Golden Means intersect.

I have already pointed out how the shape of the picture will tend to characterise the mood; you can increase this characterisation by the way you arrange the lines of the subject within the picture. Horizontal, vertical and diagonal lines are the most common. Horizontal lines give a feeling of stability, restfulness, dependability and equilibrium (Illus 39). They are particularly useful in putting over the tranquillity of a calm sea, where the picture can be made up from the horizontal lines of beach, the sea, and the sky, with perhaps a small figure or fishing boat placed on the intersection of the Golden Means.

Vertical lines give a feeling of grandeur, height, and space. In addition, if they are vertical and not tilting, they give, though to a lesser extent than horizontal lines, a feeling of stability.

The diagonal is the most powerful and dynamic line of all, because it seems to give movement to objects arranged along it (Illus 40). But be careful how you use it, for it can also give a feeling of instability, especially if unsupported by a horizontal or vertical line; and be careful not to have a diagonal line bisecting a corner of the picture. Special kinds of diagonal line are converging verticals and horizontals, which are found mainly in pictures of architecture, and in this form they give a great feeling of height or depth to your pictures.

Gently curving lines, such as rolling hills, give a feeling of smoothness, quietness, and peace. On the other hand, roughly broken lines – jagged mountain tops, for instance, or the skyline of a city – do just the opposite. They invoke feelings of tension, excitement and exhilaration.

There are only two ways in which you can learn what a good picture is and how to produce good pictures yourself. The first is by looking at other people's pictures, choosing photographers who specialise in the same type of photography in which you are interested; and the second, far more important, is by taking lots of pictures. Take a tip from the professional photographer, who rarely goes out looking for pictures in a haphazard way, but works on assignment. You can set yourself assignments in a similar way. Take an interest in a particular subject, and before you start taking pictures, read as much as you can about the subject to brief yourself, as it were, and learn what to look for when you go out with your camera. When you are ready to start shooting, study the subject from various angles and in different lights.

The professional photographer is seldom satisfied with a single photograph of a subject; instead he will take a great many, often using a whole cassette of film on one subject. This is not because he knows that if he takes enough shots, one is bound to be right, but because he knows that the more he photographs a subject, the more he will find out about it and the better his pictures will tend to become. Remember that the more pictures you take, the faster will you learn to take better pictures. Regard the film you use not as film wasted but as film *invested*. Do not be too disappointed if many of the photographs you take turn out to be not very good when you process and print them; you will find that the proportion of good ones increases quite quickly. Here is a profound thought to end the chapter with, if I may quote Ansel Adams again. He once said: 'Twelve photographs that matter in a year is a good crop for any photographer.'

Part 3 Technique

8 Exposure

Exposure is the key to the whole photographic process. If the exposure is not absolutely correct, no matter what you do subsequently, the picture will not be as good as it could be. It is one of the three bases of the photographic process, and it is interdependent with the other two – development and printing. But, in particular, exposure and development are completely inseparable. They both depend on the luminance range of the subject (the subject brightness range, as it is often called), and they both control the range of densities in the negative. On this density range depends the choice of the paper you will eventually use to print the negative. Taking matters to their logical conclusion, you should aim to expose and develop your films to produce negatives with a density range to match the exposure scale of the paper you use.

In technical terms, exposure is the product of light intensity and the time for which that intensity is effective. Both these factors must be closely controlled if a good negative is to be produced, and this is achieved with two of the basic controls on your camera – the aperture setting and the shutter speed. The first of these allows you to control the intensity of the light reaching the film and the other, the shutter speed, governs the length of time for which the light acts on the film. As both control the exposure, several combinations of aperture and shutter speed can be used to produce the same density in the negative; and the particular combination you choose will depend on the type of picture you want to produce. For example, if you are taking a shot that depends for its effect on a large depth of field, you will choose a small aperture, which will, in turn, dictate the use of a slow shutter speed, to allow the light to act

on the film for a relatively long time. On the other hand, if the picture you want to take contains fast action, you will need to use a fast shutter speed, and this will require a larger aperture, to allow more light into the camera.

One other factor comes into the determination of the correct product of shutter speed and lens aperture – the speed of the film in your camera. A slow-speed film, that is to say one with a low sensitivity, will obviously need a given intensity of light to act on it for longer than a fast film will, to produce a negative of the same density.

Before you can arrive at the correct exposure for a picture, therefore, you need to know the speed of the film and the intensity of the light. The first is supplied by the film manufacturer but the second you have to measure, and the instrument that enables you to do this is the exposure meter.

The exposure meter

This is one of the most valuable photographic tools you can have, but unless you learn to use it properly, you might just as well guess at the exposure you give your picture. What the meter tells you is how much light is reflected from your subject, or how much is falling on it – and that is all it tells you. It is then up to you to interpret this information according to the result you want, in order to arrive at the correct combination of shutter speed and aperture for that particular picture. Remember that the exposure meter is only an instrument – it cannot think for you – so use it as a guide only, and do not regard it as infallible.

Exposure meters may be either separate hand-held instruments or built into the camera. A few built-in meters are basically ordinary

hand-held meters simply integrated into the camera for convenience, and these are used in exactly the same way as the hand-held type, but an increasing number of single lens reflexes are being fitted with through-the-lens meters. Hand-held meters come in two distinct types, one working by reflected light and the other by incident light, but TTL meters work invariably by reflected light. The way in which these different types of meter are used is obvious from their names. Reflected light meters measure the amount of light reflected from an object, while incident light models measure the light falling on the object.

Hand-held meters

There are several ways of using a hand-held meter and, to a degree, they will all give you acceptable results. Let us first consider reflected light readings.

Most exposure meters are designed to indicate the exposure that will reproduce any surface you measure as a mid-grey – in fact a tone that will reflect 18 per cent of the light falling on it. This has come about because it has been calculated that if you take a general meter reading from a wide range of different subjects, all the tones in each subject will integrate more or less into a single tone that reflects 18 per cent of the light falling on it. The easiest and most common way of using a hand-held exposure meter, therefore, is to

41 If you hold the meter level when taking a general reading, the sky influences the reading too much

46 When the light is very low, you have little choice but to use a fast film such as Agfapan 1000. But the graininess often helps the picture, as in this shot of a Bradford foundry worker

The right film for the job

For pictures in which you want maximum detail, you will obviously pick a fine-grain emulsion, and since sharpness is enhanced by contrast, one with a fairly high inherent contrast. In other words, you will choose a slow film such as Agfa IF, Ilford Pan F, or Kodak Panatomic-X, and you will probably process the film in an acutance developer to increase the apparent sharpness even more.

When the level of light is low, and for indoor shots (which are often rather contrasty, especially if light sources are included in the picture), you will want the maximum speed of a fast film with its inherent softness of contrast. Films of this type include Agfa ISU, Ilford HP4, and Kodak Tri-X. In some cases the increased granularity of these films may even help in conveying the mood or atmosphere of the picture (Illus 46).

Finally, as a general purpose film, there can be little doubt that one of the medium-speed emulsions is highly suitable. They have a fair turn of speed, enough to cope with all but the lowest levels of illumination, and they are capable of resolving quite fine detail. In addition, the granularity is reasonably fine. In fact you will probably find that a film from this group – Agfa ISS, Ilford FP4, or Kodak Plus-X – will be suitable for 80 per cent of your work, unless you specialise in close-ups or candid shots in jazz clubs.

Developers and development

We have already seen that when a film is exposed in the camera, the light falling on the film partly decomposes the grains of silver halide in the emulsion. It is the fundamental job of the developer to convert these partly decomposed silver halides into metallic silver, to form the visible negative image.

Development is a complex chemical reduction process, which entails the transfer of electrons from the developer into the silver halide crystals. The precise details of how this chemical process works would be out of place in a practical book such as this, but if you are interested enough to want to know more, you can find the necessary information in any book on photographic chemistry.

The chemical that does the work of converting the silver halides into metallic silver is called the developing agent. The most popular current agents are metol, hydroquinone, and phenidone, but there are others, including amidol, pyrocatechin and glycin. These developing agents are sometimes used alone, sometimes in combination, according to the results you want. For example, metol is a soft-working developing agent that on its own produces finely graduated negatives with good shadow detail, whereas hydroquinone produces contrasty negatives. So these two agents are often used together to form one of the well known MQ developers, which give results that are neither too soft nor too contrasty. Phenidone has similar characteristics to metol, but, as it is more active, considerably less of it is needed in a given quantity of developer. It also has the advantage of not causing unpleasant skin irritation in sensitive people, which metol can do.

A simple solution of a developing agent in water will oxidise almost as soon as you mix it, so a preservative must be added to prevent this happening. The most commonly used preservative is sodium sulphite, but it does more than just slow down oxidisation: it has a solvent action on the grains of silver halide in the emulsion, causing a reduction in the granularity of the negative. Since sodium sulphite has weak alkaline properties and developing agents generally need an alkaline environment in which to work, a solution of the developing agent and sodium sulphite forms a developer, but with only very slow action (Kodak D23 is a typical example). Developers of this type have their uses where soft gradation and fine grain are required, but it is usual to speed up the action by adding a stronger alkali as an accelerator. Various alkalis are used, according to the energy required in the developer; for normal use sodium carbonate or potassium carbonate is suitable and where a high energy developer is necessary, sodium hydroxide or potassium hydroxide is a good choice. In addition to these basically fairly strong alkalis, much weaker ones are sometimes used, especially in fine-grain developers. Alkalis of this type include borax and sodium metaborate.

Finally, to prevent fogging in areas which have received little or no exposure, a restrainer is sometimes added, but in very small quantities so that it does not slow down the action of the developer unduly. Potassium bromide is the most usual restrainer, although others may be used in special cases.

Some special developers contain small quantities of other chemicals, and some do not use all the chemicals mentioned above. Most popular developers, however, are made up from a combination of these chemicals in various proportions.

Types of developer

The type of developer you use to process your films is one of the most significant factors in controlling the ultimate quality of the negative. Generally developers that are designed to extract the maximum speed out of a film are high energy solutions. Using an ultra-fine grain developer, conversely, will reduce the graininess of your negatives to the absolute minimum, but only at the expense of film speed.

Fine-grain developers Until the late 1950s or early 1960s, the inherent granularity of films was so coarse that, with a 35mm camera, you had no choice but to process your films in a fine-grain developer if you wanted to retain anything like a respectable image. At that time large numbers of special brews were available, either commercially or in the form of published formulas, which claimed to reduce the grain in your negatives to microscopic proportions. But what the manufacturers or inventors of these developers were not quite so vociferous about was the fact that they also reduced the effective speed of the films by one, two, or even more stops. So in order to retain a sensible film speed (and films in those days were considerably slower than they are now, with the fastest general-purpose emulsions around 200 ASA), you had to move into a higher speed group, where films had coarser granularity – the whole procedure became a vicious circle.

Another not so useful property of these super-fine grain developers was that they took the edge off the image sharpness of the negative by the very way in which they, and all fine grain developers, worked. To produce a graininess in a negative that is finer than the inherent granularity of the emulsion, you must obviously reduce the size of the silver halide crystals in the emulsion. This is done by using a silver solvent in the developer, and accounts for the loss of film speed; we have already seen that film speed is dependent largely on the size of the silver halide crystals. The stronger the silver solvent, the more the crystals are reduced in size and the greater the loss in film speed. As the solvent dissolves away the crystals it also dissolves away some of the sharpness of the image held within those crystals, which accounts for the very fine grain but mushy negatives produced by some of those earlier developers.

Today most of these super-fine grain developers have disappeared, with the advent of a new generation of films possessing much finer granularity and better sharpness. A good thing, too, in my opinion! However, some of the better fine grain formulas are still with us and are still extensively used. Among them is the most famous of them all, Kodak D76 (or Ilford ID11 – they are identical). In fact this formula is so widely used that it is now accepted as a general-purpose negative developer and as a standard by which all other negative developers are judged. It is made to an MQ-borax formula and produces negatives of moderately fine grain – finer than that produced by an ordinary developer but not as fine as the product of a super-fine brew. The

biggest advantage D76 has over many other standard fine grain developers is that it does not cause any loss of practical speed, and other formulas are often compared with it to give an indication of their film speed capabilities. Both D76 and ID11 are readily available in pre-packed form for mixing quantities ranging from 600cc to 15 litres or more, and this excellent availability is yet another reason for the popularity of the developer.

A particular favourite of mine among fine-grain developers is Kodak D23, which, unfortunately, is not available in pre-packed form. It is an extremely simple developer to mix up for yourself, however, and gives grain a little finer than that produced by D76. The formula is:

Metol	7.5 grammes
Sodium sulphite, anhydrous	100 grammes
Water to	1,000 cc

Development times are the same as for D76. The low alkalinity, combined with the soft-working developing agent, produces the major characteristics of the developer – a semi-compensating effect. This simply means that the developer builds up density in the shadow and mid-tone areas at a faster rate than in the highlights, a characteristic not normally found in developers containing hydroquinone as a second developing agent. The semi-compensating characteristic of D23 also makes it highly suitable for controlling the contrast of the negative, by increasing or decreasing the development time and by its use in conjunction with a separate alkali bath for very contrasty subjects.

There are a number of other proprietary fine-grain developers on the market, such as Kodak Microdol-X, Ilford Microphen, May & Baker Promicrol, Tetenal Ultrafin, and so on, all with their own claims and devotees. All these developers produce grain finer than that given by D76 and D23, but, in two cases at least, at the expense of film speed. Microphen and Promicrol, however, both give a slight increase in film speed; most unusual for this type of developer. I have tried all these developers, but have rejected them in favour of D23 and D76 for fine grain work, because I find that I do not need the reduced grain size.

Fine-grain developers are useful when you want to produce extreme enlargements from your negatives – 20 × 16in or larger from 35mm. Such developers are probably the easiest to use, since they are quite tolerant of slight over-development and over-exposure. In other words, you do not have to be quite so careful when using fine-grain developers as you do when using other types, such as the next group I am going to discuss. But you also do not get negatives of such apparent sharpness.

Acutance developers As I have already pointed out, great advances were made after the mid-1950s by photographic emulsion chemists, which resulted in a new generation of films appearing in the mid-1960s. The most noticeable effect has been a reduction in granularity without any loss in film speed; in fact, not only has the individual grain size been reduced, but the grain pattern has become more compact, too. The most important result that this has had in practical photographic terms is to make an increase in sharpness and definition possible. To make this increased sharpness even more apparent a special type of developer has become popular – the acutance developer.

Acutance developers are not new; they were first used extensively several decades ago by the German photographer Willi Beutler, who evolved a very simple formula for a soft slow-working developer. The basic Beutler formula is in two parts:

A. Metol	10 grammes
Sodium sulphite,	
anhydrous	50 grammes
Water to	1,000 cc
B. Sodium carbonate,	
anhydrous	50 grammes
Water to	1,000 cc

For use take one part of A and one part of B and add them to ten parts of water. Development times are 7–10 minutes at 20°C (68°F), and most films should be rated at twice their normal speed.

As you can see from the formula, when a working solution is mixed up, the single developing agent (metol) is in a very low concentration, as is the alkali (sodium carbonate). These proportions give two very important characteristics to the developer. Firstly, the solution is soft-working, which produces lowish general contrast – as you will remember, low contrast negatives tend to be less grainy than high contrast ones. Secondly, the low alkalinity prevents the developer penetrating deeply into the emulsion, so that most of the development takes place on or near the surface of the emulsion. This reduces irradiation so increasing sharpness. It also reduces overlapping of grain clumps at different levels in the emulsion, giving apparently finer grain.

By keeping the agitation to the minimum, Willi Beutler found that in the highlight areas of the negative, which produce heavy deposits of silver, the developer became exhausted very much more quickly than in the thinner shadow areas. This results in a compensating effect, where the highlight areas are held down in density while the shadows are allowed

to build up to give added detail in these important areas. Since the speed of a film is determined by measuring the amount of exposure necessary to produce a certain density of silver at the toe of the characteristic curve – corresponding to a shadow area – this increased shadow detail means that you actually get an increase in effective film speed.

The Beutler developer, then, gives fine-grain, increased shadow detail without blocking up the highlights, and an increase in effective film speed. But the combination of low developing agent concentration and minimum agitation gives yet another advantage, possibly the most important of all. In areas where there are rapid changes from light to dark tone – areas with a great deal of fine detail – the edges between the light and dark tones appear to be much sharper than when the film is processed in a conventional developer. This is caused by exhausted developer in the dark areas seeping over into the light areas and retarding development locally. At the same time, relatively fresh developer from the light areas seeps over into the darker areas and boosts development locally, resulting in an increase in contrast at the point where the light and dark tones meet. The effect of the Beutler developer, therefore, is to give low general contrast (sometimes called macro-contrast) with fairly high detail contrast (micro-contrast), a characteristic that holds true for all acutance developers.

Several proprietary acutance developers are available, the oldest established being Neofin from the German chemical firm of Tetenal. This appeared in 1945 as a direct result of collaboration between Tetenal and Willi Beutler; Neofin in fact is a modified version of the original Beutler formula. It is available in two types, Neofin Blue for slow and medium-speed films and Neofin Red for faster films. Other acutance developers are Paterson Acutol and Acuspecial, both of which are non-Beutler types and claim better gradation and contrast control. Both these developers, together with other types in the Paterson range, were formulated by the British photographer Geoffrey Crawley.

Acutance developers are the most generally suitable for modern small format films, and I use them for most of my black and white work. For the rest I tend to use D76, D23, or a two-bath developer.

Two-bath developers One of the problems with using conventional fine grain developers is that the developing agents become progressively exhausted, and, for each film processed, by-products (mostly in the form of potassium bromide) are thrown out into the developer. These tend to slow down the action of the solution, which means that you have to increase the development time for every film after the first if you want consistent results. In addition, you are never *quite* sure just when the developer is finally exhausted. This is the prime reason for using acutance developers, which are invariably one-shot brews, giving completely consistent results.

An alternative answer to this problem of progressive exhaustion is to use one solution for the developing agent and another for the alkali. The film is placed first in the solution containing the developing agent and a preservative. Little or no development takes place in this solution, the film merely becoming saturated with the developer, but the developing agent in the remaining solution does not become exhausted. Every film, therefore, becomes saturated with fresh developer and consistent results are achieved.

Development proper takes place in the second solution – the alkali bath. The developer with which the film has become saturated in the first bath is activated by the alkali in the second bath, and development to completion takes place quite rapidly. For completely consistent results, the alkali bath should be used once only and then discarded, but since it consists only of a few grammes of borax in water, it is very cheap.

The action of the two-bath developer gives several important benefits. Firstly, because development takes place only when the absorbed developer has been activated by the alkali solution, no further development can take place when that developer becomes exhausted. This means that the developer in the highlight areas becomes exhausted fairly rapidly, whereas that in the shadows works more slowly, giving a compensating action that is particularly useful for contrasty subjects. In fact, by altering the time in the first bath, so regulating the amount of developer absorbed by the film, you can control the contrast of your negatives quite finely.

Secondly, the effective speed of the film is not reduced noticeably. In fact if anything the effective speed is increased slightly due to the increased shadow detail. Next, since the development takes place at or near the surface of the emulsion there is a marked reduction in both halation and irradiation compared with conventional fine grain developers. This also makes for increased image sharpness. Then, because development is continued to the exhaustion point of the developer absorbed by the emulsion in the first bath, temperature is not critical. Neither is the time in the second bath, provided it is long enough to activate fully the developer absorbed by the film. And finally, a point which is becoming increasingly important with rising prices, both

baths of this developer are cheap to make up and economical in use.

There are several formulas available for two-bath developer. My preference is for D23 as the first bath and a 2 per cent solution of borax (made by dissolving 20 grammes of borax in a litre of water) as the second bath. Development times will naturally vary according to the type of negatives you prefer, but the following gives a good indication. First bath: 3 minutes for slow films, 4 minutes for medium-speed films, and 6–7 minutes for fast films. Second bath: 1 minute for all films. The film should be agitated continuously in the first bath, but left as still as possible in the second. My own method is to pour out the first bath after the appropriate time, allowing about 20 seconds for the tank to drain, then pour in the second bath and put the tank down carefully. After 15 seconds I invert the tank and stand it on its lid, after a further 15 seconds I invert it again so that it is back on its base, and after yet another 15 seconds I remove the lid and invert the tank to begin draining. This method avoids the uneven development that would occur if the tank was left completely alone, while also avoiding the dispersion of the absorbed developer that would occur if the film was agitated continuously.

If you do not have the facilities for mixing up your own developers, or if you cannot persuade your local chemist to do it for you, use the one proprietary two-bath developer that is available. This is Emofin, made by the German Tetenal company, which works in a similar way to D23 and borax solution. Detailed instructions are, of course, included in the pack.

Developing your films

The development of black and white negative films is often regarded far too lightly, too little attention being paid to accurate time and temperature control, to agitation, and to the condition of the developer itself. Inevitably the result is inconsistent negative quality, and if you have inconsistent negatives, you can hardly expect to produce consistent prints.

For consistent negatives, I would personally recommend the use of one-shot developers whenever possible. In this way you can be absolutely sure that every tankful of developer you use is fresh, uncontaminated by the accumulated by-products of previous processing. I would also suggest that you standardise on agitation, and use a certified thermometer and a stop-watch or seconds timer for accurate time and temperature control.

Agitation is an important part of development: too much, and the film becomes overdeveloped and loses sharpness; too little, and

47 This subject, while lit by average light, was inherently low in contrast, so an increased development time was given to add a little punch

uneven development and streaking result. Use only inversion agitation. It has been shown that rotary agitation is not completely even, giving unequal development across the width of the film. Pour the developer into the tank, using no more than the manufacturer specifies, and invert the tank back and forth continuously for a full 15 seconds. Then set the tank down and let it stand untouched until the end of the first minute of the development time. Give one complete inversion – over and back – every minute until the end of the development time, but do not forget to allow about 20 seconds to drain the tank before the development time is up.

For the control of temperature, as distinct from checking the temperature, I stand the tank in a bowl of water kept at the correct temperature by a dish heater. Once this relatively large mass of water has reached the correct temperature, it has enough thermal inertia to maintain it for the length of the development time.

Development times The development times recommended by film and developer manufacturers in their data sheets and instruction slips are correct only for so-called average subjects in average lighting conditions. In other words, the recommended development time is a compromise intended to give acceptable results under a wide variety of conditions. If you want to produce optimum results you must take the manufacturer's recommended time as a guide only, and modify this time when either the subject or the lighting conditions depart from average.

Subject luminance ranges vary considerably. On the one hand you have brilliantly lit subjects with exceedingly bright highlights and deep black shadows, and on the other you have flat misty conditions where the brightest highlights are a light grey and the deepest shadows are a slightly darker grey. Between these two extremes lies a vast range of other subject types and lighting conditions, so that it is obviously quite difficult to decide just what constitutes an average subject. Perhaps the closest approach is a sunny landscape with no large areas of extreme highlight or shadow, a subject that probably has a luminance range of about five stops (32 : 1). It is on this type of subject that film and developer manufacturers base their development time recommendations.

But what happens when you photograph subjects with much higher or lower luminance ranges? If you process and print the negatives in the usual way, you will produce prints that are very much below standard. Subjects with a long luminance range will give contrasty negatives which, on normal grade paper, will

produce harsh prints with solid black shadows and burnt-out highlights. The answer, at first glance, seems to be to print these negatives on a much softer grade of paper. This will help, of course, but only in part; it will not separate out the highlight and shadow tones to give added detail, for the detail is simply not there in the original negative. The opposite is true of subjects with a short luminance range. They will produce flat negatives which, on normal paper, give weak prints lacking in clear whites and full blacks. This time you can improve matters by printing on a harder grade of paper, but again the print will lack detail in the shadows and highlights.

For optimum quality in both negatives and prints, there is only one really satisfactory answer. You must modify the development time to suit the luminance range of the subject. Before you can decide how much to modify the development time, and in what direction, you must measure the luminance range of the subject as I have described in the chapter on exposure. When you have done this, you can make a note to increase the development time to compensate for subjects of low luminance range or to decrease it for those with high luminance range. In this way you can produce consistent negatives that will all print on a single grade of paper.

The exact amount by which you need to increase or decrease the development time will depend on the actual luminance range of the subject; Table 2 will give you some idea of the extent to which you can control contrast in this way. Although development time primarily controls the contrast of a negative, it obviously also has some effect on the density of the image, especially if the development time is cut by more than about 25 per cent. Table 2 also gives the amount by which you must modify the effective film speed to allow for this.

Table 2

Subject luminance range	Speed rating modification	Development time (per cent increase or decrease on 100)
10 : 1	$+\frac{1}{3}$ stop	200
20 : 1	$+\frac{1}{3}$ stop	150
40 : 1	Normal	100
100 : 1	$-\frac{2}{3}$ stop	80
250 : 1	-1 stop	70
500 : 1	-2 stops	60
1,000 : 1	-3 stops	50

I must stress, however, that the figures in this table are only a guide, and for optimum results you should carry out tests with your

48 When the subject contrast is high, as in these lock gates, a reduction in development time can help

usual films and developers to find out the best ratings and development times for your particular working methods.

For subjects with long luminance ranges – more than 250 : 1 – the use of a two-bath developer will give the best results. With a conventional developer used for a reduced time, the shadow areas do not get time to build up to a usable density, with the result that they tend to block up in the print. The way in which a two-bath developer works prevents this from happening, because, once the developer in the highlight areas has become exhausted, no amount of further time in the second bath will produce more density in the highlights. By reducing the immersion time in the first bath, therefore, you can control the amount of developer absorbed by the film and limit the highlight densities while the shadows are allowed to build up. Table 3 gives suitable starting points for experiment with high luminance ranges.

Table 3

Subject luminance range	First bath time (mins)			Second bath time (mins)
	Slow films	Medium-speed films	Fast films	All films
40 : 1	3	4	6	1
100 : 1	$2\frac{2}{3}$	$3\frac{1}{2}$	5	1
250 : 1	$2\frac{1}{3}$	3	4	1
500 : 1	2	$2\frac{1}{2}$	3	1
1,000 : 1	$1\frac{1}{2}$	$1\frac{3}{4}$	2	1

All this talk of matching development time to subject luminance range is fine as long as all the shots on a roll of film are taken at the same time or under similar conditions. Unfortunately, though, this does not always happen, and can create problems. However, with 35mm films you can always cut an exposed length of film off in the darkroom and give it one type of development, keeping the rest of the film for a different type of subject needing a different treatment. But if the range of subject contrasts falls between about 20 : 1 and 100 : 1, the best course of action is probably to give normal development and use two or three grades of paper to compensate at the printing stage.

Temperature The temperature of the developer is a very important factor in film processing: if the developer is too warm, the effect is the same as developing the film for too long; if it is too cool, the effect is of under-development. Most developers are designed for use at 20°C (68°F), but you can use them without any special precautions at temperatures ranging from 17°C (62°F) to 24°C (76°F). Below 17°C the developing agents may not reach full activity, and above 24°C the emulsion on the film may soften to the point where it starts frilling. Even though you can use developers over this range, you must modify the development time to allow for the change in temperature from the standard. A good rule of thumb is to increase or decrease the development time by 10 per cent for every 1°C (2°F) the temperature is below or above the standard of 20°C (68°F).

Developing tanks Nearly all modern developing tanks are designed for inversion agitation, and, as I mentioned earlier, this is the only type of agitation you should use. The tanks are available in plastic or stainless steel, and both have features to recommend them. Plastic tanks are generally inexpensive, and modern ones are highly resistant to accidental damage by dropping and excess heat. They also retain heat well, so that on a cold day the temperature of the developer does not drop quickly. But they are sometimes difficult to load, especially with wet film during colour processing, and can be awkward to dry thoroughly if you want to process two films one after the other. However, most plastic spirals are transparent, to eliminate the need for the wet film to be removed and reloaded during colour processing.

A good stainless steel tank is quite expensive, but it will outlast several plastic ones. The reels invariably load from the centre, and are equally easy to load wet or dry. Stainless steel conducts heat more easily than plastic, so that developer in a steel tank tends to drop in temperature rapidly on a cold day. But it is equally rapid in transferring heat from warm water to the developer to raise the temperature again. Usually there are no complicated mouldings on a stainless steel tank to make drying difficult, but, as the spirals are easy to load when wet, this is of little consequence anyway.

Personally I use both stainless steel and plastic tanks, and find them equally convenient. But I tend to keep the stainless steel ones for black and white work, and the plastic tanks, because of their transparent spirals, for colour.

One or two tanks use a very small amount of developer, and in them the film spiral is in a horizontal position rather than a vertical one. The idea is that only part of the film is in the developer at any one time, and to ensure uniform development, the spiral has to be turned continuously. As far as I am concerned, these tanks have nothing at all to recommend them. Their need for continuous agitation nullifies the action of acutance developers, which depend on minimum agitation to create the beneficial edge effect. Because they use such small amounts of solution, there is the risk of the developer becoming exhausted before the completion of development. Finally, since the agitation is rotary, there is the constant danger of streaking and uneven development.

After development When the development process is complete, the action of the developer must be halted as quickly as possible by means of a stop bath. Since developers are alkaline in composition, the quickest way to stop their action is by neutralising them with a weak acid. The most common stop bath, therefore, is a simple 2 per cent solution of acetic acid. There are also proprietary stop baths on the market, some of which contain an indicator that changes colour when the stop bath has lost its activity. The use of a stop bath also increases the life of the fixer, because little or no alkaline developer is carried over to neutralise the fixing bath.

After the stop bath has been poured out of the developing tank, fixer is poured in. Fixer is simply a solution of silver solvent – sodium thiosulphate or ammonium thiosulphate – which removes all the unexposed and undeveloped silver halides in the emulsion, leaving these areas as clear film. In its simplest form the fixer is an approximate 10 per cent solution of sodium thiosulphate, which is quite adequate in most cases. But additives are usually included to make the fixer more effective and to make it do more. Sodium or potassium metabisulphite is often added as an acidifying agent to neutralise the developer if a stop bath has not been used, or if any developer is still retained in the emulsion after the stop bath. To harden the emulsion and protect it against

scratching during subsequent handling, potassium aluminium sulphate (alum) is often added.

All residual chemicals must be removed from the film to avoid the risk of staining, and this is done by washing the film, still in its spiral, for 20 to 30 minutes in water. The most efficient way is to use a force washer, which jets water in through the tank lid, down to the bottom of the tank, and back up through the film and spiral, to flow out at the top of the tank, taking the chemicals with it. It is advisable to use a water filter to prevent minute particles of dirt getting on to the film, for they could cause white spots when you make your prints.

As a final step before drying, let your film soak in fresh filtered water containing a few drops of wetting agent. This helps to speed drying, and prevents the streaky appearance you sometimes get when a film has dried unevenly. Some photographers advise the use of a film wiper to remove surplus water, but I never do, because there is always the risk of a particle of grit becoming trapped in the wiper blade and scratching the film. Instead I just hang my films up and the surplus water very quickly drains off the bottom.

When your films are hanging up to dry, try to disturb the air around them as little as possible. You will not then stir up dust, which could stick to the wet emulsion and cause you spotting problems later.

10 Colour in Your SLR

The first question you must ask yourself when you decide to take a picture in colour is, 'Why colour?'. As far as most people are concerned, the answer to that one is that colour photographs are more natural than black and white pictures. Because there is colour all around us all the time, colour photographs give a more realistic representation of the subject in front of us; a black and white picture is, by its very nature, an abstraction of the real thing. Yet, paradoxically, a colour photograph does not always give the most satisfactory results, simply because the colour is used in the wrong way. It contributes nothing to the picture and is being used simply for its own sake. So the answer to the 'Why colour?' question must be that, for the picture you are about to take, colour is an essential part of the composition; without it the picture would fail to hold together. If you cannot give this answer to the question, the picture will almost certainly be a failure as a colour shot, and may well be more successful as a black and white shot.

Prints or slides?

Basically there are two types of colour film, negative and reversal. Negative colour films are used in exactly the same way as black and white films and you make, or have made for you, colour prints on paper from the negatives. Reversal films, on the other hand, produce a picture direct in the form of a transparency, which you project on to a screen or look at in a viewer or light box. Both types have advantages and disadvantages.

From a colour negative you can make as many colour prints as you like, and transparencies on print film, too, if necessary. Even black and white prints are fairly easy to produce. But with reversal film the single transparency produced by the film is unique and quite irreplaceable. It is true that you can make duplicate transparencies from it, and prints in colour or black and white, but the quality of these is almost always inferior to that of the original.

The problem of quality also forms the main disadvantage of the negative-positive colour process. No matter how good a colour print is, it can never approach the transparency for sheer quality. This is because a transparency, viewed by transmitted light, is capable of reproducing a much longer tone range than a print that is viewed by reflected light. Even the very deepest black on a print will reflect some 2 per cent of the light falling on it, and the brightest clear white highlights will only reflect about 80 per cent, so the maximum brightness range you can possibly achieve in a colour print is only about 40 : 1.

Under good projection conditions – a very dark room, a powerful projection lamp, and a glass-beaded screen for maximum reflectance – the brightness range of a colour transparency can be 100 : 1 or even more. But a projected image is still reflected from the screen, so this brightness range can be increased still further by viewing the transparency by direct transmitted light, as in a viewer or on a light box. Under such conditions it is possible to reproduce a brightness range of 300 : 1 or more.

One of the main disadvantages of colour transparencies is that special arrangements have to be made for viewing them, either by setting up a projector and screen or by passing a viewer around the group of people to whom you are showing the pictures. With colour prints, however, you can simply put a handful of them in your pocket and pass them round quite easily and without fuss. If you make large colour prints and mount them for display, you can hang them on the walls of your living room to be looked at any time.

But probably the main disadvantage of the reversal film is the lack of control you have over the final result, compared with the negative-positive process. Once you have exposed the film and processed it, there is very little you can do about the result. With the negative-positive process, though, the colour negative is only the start of things. In the darkroom you can control very closely the results you get in the finished print. By careful filtration you can intensify certain colours and weaken others; you can burn in parts of the image just as in black and white printing; you can alter the colour balance of small areas of the print by local control.

The type of colour film you choose, then, depends on what you want to do with the finished pictures. If you want the convenience of colour prints and the opportunity of controlling the result at the printing stage, and are prepared to put up with the deficiencies of colour prints, you will choose a colour negative film. But if you want the ultimate in colour quality, and prefer to view your pictures projected on to a screen, then reversal film will be your choice.

Exposure for colour

The colour of an object has three basic characteristics: hue, saturation, and tone or brightness. Accurate reproduction of a colour depends on getting the balance of these three characteristics the same in the picture as they are in the subject.

Hue is the actual colour of an object – blue, green, yellow, etc – and the reproduction of hue depends on the colour of the light falling on the object when you make your exposure. The saturation and tone of a colour, however, both depend on the *amount* of light falling on the object. This means that the reproduction of both saturation and tone can be controlled by the exposure you give when you take the picture.

Colour films, especially colour reversal films, have very much less exposure latitude than black and white films, taking latitude in the broadest meaning of the word. Often it is less than one stop either side of the correct exposure, compared with sometimes as much as three stops either way with a black and white film. So you obviously have to be much more accurate in determining exposure for colour work than for black and white.

When you are projecting a series of colour slides, it is very disconcerting for your audience if the highlight brightness of consecutive slides keeps changing. It is much more accept-able if the highlights remain at a reasonably constant brightness from one slide to another, and the way to ensure this is to base the exposures for your transparencies on highlight readings. The most consistently accurate way to do this is by using the incident light method of taking a meter reading, as explained in Chapter 8, p 91.

Since colour film has so little latitude you must calibrate the film you use to suit your particular camera and exposure meter. This is quite simply a matter of taking a series of five shots of the same subject at different exposures. First determine the exposure in your usual way with the meter set to the recommended film speed, and expose the first frame of the film at the shutter speed and aperture indicated by the meter. Now repeat the shot with the lens aperture opened by half a stop, and again with the lens opened a full stop. Take two more shots, this time with the lens closed down half a stop and a full stop from the indicated exposure. The subject for this test should be one with a good range of colours and tones, and lit from the front or slightly to one side. Perhaps the most suitable subject of all is a person holding a set of colour patches, such as a paint manufacturer's colour chart, and either a grey scale or a piece of grey card.

When the film has been processed, select the transparency which gives the best reproduction of the test subject. If this is any but the first frame of your series (the frame exposed according to your exposure meter's recommendation), you will know that you need to rate the film at a speed different from that recommended by the manufacturer. But this will apply only to the film in *your* camera, exposed according to *your* means of exposure measurement, with *your* exposure meter. If you use the same film in another camera, you may find that you have to rate it differently again. These differences are likely to be quite small: for instance, in my Prakticamat I have to rate Ektachrome-X, which Kodak say is 64 ASA, at 80 ASA or I get over-exposed transparencies. The change is only a third of a stop, but it makes a big difference to the results. If you are striving for the best possible transparencies, it is small errors like this that can prevent you from achieving your aim.

Back to the test. If you are using a film that the manufacturer says should be rated at 50 ASA, and the fourth frame of the test series is the most satisfactory, you will need to rate the film at 64 ASA for your particular combination of camera and meter; or if the best shot is the third in the series, you must rate the film at 25 ASA.

It is most important that you judge the results of the test under suitable conditions.

Best of all is to project them in a well darkened room, but a good alternative is to put them in a viewer indirectly illuminated by a piece of white card, which is in turn lit by a 100–150W tungsten lamp.

A side effect of these tests is that they enable you to see exactly what happens when a film is over- or under-exposed, and you can use this information to guide you for future pictures – as a creative control over the tones in the picture. Basically, over-exposure produces lighter tones and less saturated colours whereas under-exposure darkens the tones and increases the saturation of the colours. For controlling tones and saturation, an exposure deviation of half a stop either way from the meter indication is usually sufficient, but for the occasional subject a whole stop may be necessary.

If you are in any doubt at all about the correct exposure to give, it is worth bracketing. This simply means that you take three shots of your subject instead of one. The first of these is at the indicated exposure and the other two at half stops more and less than the indicated exposure. In this way you are almost certain to get one correctly exposed transparency. Of course, it increases the cost of the picture threefold, but that is much better than losing the picture altogether. If it is a really tricky shot, it may be worth taking a further two pictures a whole stop either side of the indicated exposure.

Lighting for colour

Generally speaking, you cannot, if you are taking pictures out of doors, control the intensity, direction, quality, or colour of the light. These are all determined by the prevailing conditions, so that all you can do is adapt your exposure and technique to those conditions.

The intensity of the light is the easiest characteristic to deal with, because you simply measure it with your exposure meter and use the information given by the meter to set your camera controls. Light intensity does not affect the reproduction of colours in your transparencies too much. Obviously, if you take a picture in the bright glaring light of the mid-day sun, the colours will be brighter and more saturated than if you take the picture on an overcast day, but this is more a question of the quality of the light rather than its intensity.

When you take a black and white picture, you rely on the contrasts between tones to give your pictures form. This means that you mostly need a fairly bright light source to produce highlights and shadows. Colour photographs, on the other hand, do not need these contrasts in tones to give them form, because they have colour itself to do the job in a much stronger way.

For colour photographs, then, bright lighting is not so important as it is for black and white photography; in fact it can, in some cases, be a distinct embarrassment. While a colour transparency is capable of reproducing a brightness range of 300 : 1 or even more, this range extends from clear film to the maximum density of which the film is capable. Detail is recorded in a much smaller range – much smaller, in fact, than in a black and white negative. For this reason you must keep a very careful eye on the brightness range of your subject.

In landscapes or architectural pictures the problem is not great. If the shadows form the greater part of the picture, it does not matter too much if the highlights are over-exposed to the point where they burn out. If the highlights are the major part of the picture, small shadows can safely be left to fill in. However, if you are taking a portrait or a flower study, deep black shadows or burnt-out highlights are very distracting, so the lighting should be much softer for this type of picture. Cloudy or overcast conditions are ideal. If you are rather doubtful of the validity of this piece of advice, try a simple test. Take a portrait or a flower study in bright sunlit conditions and repeat the shot on a cloudy day, then see which you find more pleasing. I think it will be the second shot. The reason for this is quite simple. The layer of cloud acts as a diffuser to produce an immense light source that in turn gives soft shadows and delicate highlights well within the recording capabilities of the film. If the picture is a portrait, you have the additional advantage that your model will not be squinting to overcome the glare of the bright sunlight.

Beginners are often advised to take their pictures with the sun behind them, to give flat frontal lighting. About the only thing that can be said for this advice is that it is safe. But it produces boring pictures. So the best thing is to forget it.

If you are taking pictures on a cloudy day, there is not much you can do about the direction of the light, for, however you move around your subject, the direction of the light will always be from the top. But, as I have already pointed out, this soft lighting is ideal for most colour work.

If the conditions are sunny, however, and you can move around your subject, you can use the direction of the lighting to your advantage. Possibly the most universally useful lighting angle is around 45° to one side of the subject. This produces small shadows to emphasise texture, and gives pleasing moulding to smooth shapes. More pronounced textural effects can be obtained by altering the viewpoint so that the direction of the light

Noon

Atmosphere

Evening

Morning

49 This drawing illustrates why daylight is much redder in the early morning and late evening than at noon. The light at these times has to penetrate a much thicker layer of atmosphere than at noon, and the atmosphere diffuses the blue component of the light

is fully to one side of the subject, and if you want to add real drama, shoot straight into the light. This can be particularly effective in the early morning or late evening, when the sun is low and can be included in the picture. In these cases, though, exposure becomes very critical; it is best to take a reflected highlight reading or a reading direct from the sun and let the shadows look after themselves.

Colour of light Quite apart from the difference in the angles of lighting throughout the day, there is a big difference in the colour of the light, too. Early in the morning and late in the evening the light is much redder than it is at mid-day. This phenomenon is quite easy to explain (Illus 49). Just after sunrise and just before sunset the sun's rays have to pass through considerably more of the earth's atmosphere than when the sun is overhead at noon. Since the atmosphere, which in addition to air, is composed of dust, water vapour, smoke, and so on, filters out a proportion of the blue content of the light, the sun appears to be much redder at sunrise and sunset.

The human eye compensates for this difference in colour of the light source, so that an object which appears, say, green at mid-day also appears green early in the morning or late in the evening. It even appears green in artificial light, which is redder than daylight even at these times. But the trouble is that colour films are not like our eyes. A film sees colour the way it really is, not the way we would like it to be, so it records an object with a pronounced red cast at sunrise and sunset and without it at noon. To produce pictures of objects in their true colours, then, you need to correct the colour of the light as it enters your camera, but, before I go into this, a few words about colour film balance are necessary.

If you use a colour film in lighting conditions that are different from those for which it was designed, you will get a general change in the colour reproduction – a colour cast. Colour films fall basically into two types – those designed for use in daylight and those intended for artificial light use – and the three layers of emulsion making up the film are balanced accordingly. This is achieved by making the speeds of the three layers the same to light of a specific colour. A daylight film has its three layers at the same effective speed when it is exposed to daylight at midday or a couple of hours either side. Expose this film to an artificial light source and you upset this balance. The effective speed of the red-sensitive emulsion layer increases while that of the blue-sensitive layer drops. As the red-sensitive layer produces a cyan image and the blue-sensitive layer a yellow one, this means that, after processing, the cyan image will be of low density while the yellow image is high in density, giving a reddish-orange cast to the whole transparency. The opposite effect occurs if you expose film balanced for artificial light to a subject lit by daylight.

Colour temperature The colour of any light source can be expressed in two ways – as a colour temperature in degrees Kelvin or in mireds. The units usually quoted are degrees Kelvin, but those that are easier to use for photographic purposes are mireds.

'Mired' is made up from the words micro-reciprocal degree; the mired colour temperature of a light source is equal to one million divided by the degree Kelvin colour temperature. For example, a colour temperature of $5,800°K$, which is that of summer noon sunlight, has a mired value of $1,000,000/5,800 = 172$.

I have explained how daylight can vary in colour from very red at sunrise and sunset to very blue skylight. This range extends, in fact, from a colour temperature as low as $2,500°K$ (400 mireds) just after sunrise, right up to $26,000°K$ (38 mireds) for very clear blue sky lighting shadows. A colour film can only be balanced for one specific colour temperature and that, for daylight films, is usually around $6,000°K$ (167 mireds). When the light-

ing is more than 10 or 15 mireds different from this colour temperature, red or blue colour casts start to appear. To cancel these out, you need to use a correction filter on your camera lens.

Filters for colour Even when the colour temperature of the lighting is the same as that for which the film is balanced, it is worth using an ultra-violet (UV) absorbing filter, because there is nearly always a large amount of UV in daylight. You cannot see it, but the film can, and it sees it as blue. What we are more concerned with here, though, is using filters to correct colour casts.

The difference between the colour temperature of the light source in mireds and that of the film you are using, also in mireds, is called the mired shift. The object of using a filter is to reduce this mired shift to zero or to as small a figure as possible. To achieve this, you use a filter of the same mired value but of opposite colour to the mired shift. An example will make this clear.

Assume you are using Ektachrome-X, which is balanced for $5,500°K$ (182 mireds), and you want to take a picture in cloudy conditions of $8,000°K$ (125 mireds). You must always subtract the mired value of the film from that of the light source and not the other way round. This then tells you whether the mired shift is positive or negative. A negative mired shift means that the colour temperature of the light source is higher than that of the film and vice versa. So in this example the mired shift is -57, and needs a positive mired filter to correct it.

Correction filters are either reddish or bluish. The red filters have positive values and the blue negative. They are usually available in four densities – 15, 30, 60, and 120 mireds – and are coded with a prefix letter R or B. Some manufacturers quote the densities of their filters in decamireds (tens of mireds), and in this case the filters would be numbered $1\frac{1}{2}$, 3, 6, and 12 respectively.

Going back to our example, a filter of $+57$ mireds is needed to correct the blue cast produced by the lighting. The plus sign tells us that the filter needs to be red, and the nearest standard filter is R60 or R6. This will correct the colour cast to within 3 mireds, which will be almost impossible to detect in the transparency.

Colour temperature correction filters, like any other filters, are quite expensive, so that it will obviously cost you a lot of money to buy a complete set of eight, especially if all your lenses take different sizes. I have found that the most useful filters to have are R15, R30, R60, B30 and B120. These enable me to handle practically all daylight conditions as well as using daylight film in artificial light if I have to. Colour correction filters are additive, so this basic set gives you a wider range of corrections that is obvious at first glance. The R15 and R30, for instance, can be used together to correct a mired shift of −45. But remember that if you use more than two filters together, you increase the risk of flare and loss of contrast.

Naturally you should only use colour temperature correction filters if you want a neutral colour balance in your transparencies. For example, if you are shooting a sunset where the whole picture depends on the dramatic redness, do not use a correction filter or you will completely ruin the atmosphere of the picture.

Although the most satisfactory way to determine the colour temperature of a light source is by using a special colour temperature meter, these are quite costly, and unless you take only colour pictures, the cost may not be justified. So I have included a set of tables in the appendices of this book to enable you to choose the right filter. Obviously these tables are not as accurate as a colour temperature meter, but they will give you a good approximation.

11 Printing Your Negatives

Printing is the ultimate step in black and white photography because the print is what other people see of your photography and must stand or fall on its own merits. These people looking at your pictures want results, not excuses, so you must do your best to give them results. But in addition to being one of the most satisfying of photographic processes, printing is also the most complicated, with so many different facets. It is, therefore, impossible to cover the subject in real depth in a single chapter, and I suggest that you read my book *Practical Photographic Enlarging* for full details about printing, including the selection of equipment and the setting up of a darkroom.

In Chapters 8 and 9 I explained how to expose and develop your films properly to produce technically perfect negatives, which are the first steps towards producing perfect prints. The other requirements are the correct type and grade of paper, the correct exposure of the paper in the enlarger, and the correct processing of the print. Before dealing with these aspects, let us have a look at the basic equipment you need for printing.

Equipment

You do not need much to start printing. In fact you can get by with an enlarger, a safelight, a thermometer, and two or three dishes.

Enlargers An enlarger must be mechanically and optically sound if you are to produce satisfactory prints. The definition and resolution of the fine detail in your prints depends as much on the quality of your enlarger lens as on that of your camera lens. To get the maximum sharpness in your prints, your en-larger lens must be at least as good as the lens in your camera.

Other things to look for when you buy an enlarger are a good rigid column; a sturdy focusing mechanism; a well-made negative carrier that will hold the negative perfectly flat, and preferably with built-in masking; an adequately ventilated lamphouse; and a perfectly flat and solid base-board that does not rock. Check that the base-board, lens panel and negative carrier are parallel, or you will have unevenly focused, distorted prints.

If you think that you may progress to colour printing later on, it is worth buying an enlarger with a filter drawer or a colour head ready for this. It will cost you more to have the enlarger converted later than to buy this fitment as original equipment.

Safelight So that you can see your way around in your darkroom, you will need a safelight, which, for black and white printing, is an orange- or lime-coloured light to which the emulsion on the printing paper is insensitive. There is one type of safelight on the market, made by Paterson, which will hang from the ceiling or on a wall, or stand on a flat surface. This is ideal if your darkroom is fairly small or temporary. But if you want to do things other than black and white printing, calling for safelights of different colours, you will do better to buy one that takes standard interchangeable screens. These are available in various sizes up to about 10 by 8in, but for a small darkroom the Kodak Beehive safelight is difficult to beat.

50 A good medium-priced enlarger for 35mm negatives, made by Paterson

Thermometer You should already have bought a good accurate thermometer for processing your films, and this is equally suitable for printing. However, if you want to keep a separate instrument for printing, there are one or two thermometers designed especially for use in developing dishes. Since you will be developing your prints by inspection, your thermometer for printing need not be as accurate as the one you use for your film processing.

Dishes Most dishes these days are made from plastic, which has almost entirely replaced the enamelled steel of the earlier dishes, which are now very expensive. The plastic type have several advantages anyway: they are impervious to chemicals; they will not chip, as enamelled steel dishes will; and if you do happen to split one, it is relatively cheap to replace. Buy a large dish for your fixer, so that the prints can move about easily; for developer and stop bath buy a pair of 10×8in dishes and, if you intend to make large prints occasionally, add a pair of 15×12in dishes as well.

This is all the basic equipment you need to start enlarging, but as you go along you will probably want to add to it with items such as print forceps to keep your fingers out of the chemicals, measures, an enlarger exposure meter to make exposure determination faster and easier, an electronic timer to control the enlarger, and so on.

Darkroom Obviously it is highly desirable to have a permanent darkroom fitted out with benches, cupboards and hot and cold running water, but this is a luxury available to few amateur photographers. So you will have to make your prints in a temporary darkroom. Any room that can be efficiently blacked out is suitable. If it does not have running water, you can put your prints in a bucket of water when they have fixed and wash them in the bath later. But remember, if you are using the bathroom as your temporary darkroom, photographic equipment and materials can deteriorate quickly in a damp atmosphere, so take all your kit out to somewhere drier when you have finished your printing session.

Choosing the paper

Printing papers for enlarging are made in two basic types – bromide and chlorobromide. Bromide papers produce prints with neutral black tones tending, if anything, towards coolness, while chlorobromide papers produce warm black tones. Both types of paper are available in a variety of surfaces, although in recent years most manufacturers have rationalised their ranges and offer less choice than they did. I prefer to use only glossy paper. Because its surface is smooth, a glossy paper will always produce prints that are sharper than those on a textured paper surface. The maximum black possible on a glossy paper is better than that on any other surface, especially if you glaze the print. Finally, glossy paper offers a choice of two paper surfaces: by allowing it to dry naturally or face up on an electric print dryer you produce prints with a smooth sheen finish, and by glazing the print you can achieve a high gloss finish.

Most papers are available in two thicknesses – single weight and double weight. You will find that, for most purposes, single weight paper is adequate, and as it is considerably less expensive than double weight, you can save quite a lot of money over a period of a year or so. Although many papers are available in a choice of white, ivory or cream base, I would strongly advise against using anything except white; if you use a paper with a coloured base, you cannot possibly get the same sparkle in the highlights as you can on a white paper.

The right grade The real secret of printing is to match the paper on which you make the print to the negative – in other words, choosing the correct grade of paper. This choice is governed by the range of negative densities you want to reproduce in the print: if you want to reproduce all the tones in the negative, the contrast scale of the paper must equal, more or less, the density range of the negative. Let us look at an example. Consider a negative with a minimum density of 0.6 and a maximum density of 1.6, giving a density range of 1.0 or 10 : 1. If your standard grade of paper has a contrast scale of, say, 1–4 or 25 : 1, it is obvious that the range of densities in the negative will not fill the contrast scale of the paper. So one of two things will happen. If you expose the paper sufficiently to just produce a tone in the area of the print that corresponds to the maximum density area of the negative, the maximum black in the print will be only a dark grey; or if your printing exposure is sufficient to give a full black from the minimum density area of the negative, the lightest areas of the print will be light grey. But whichever the result you produce, the print will be flat and lacking in life.

Alternatively, if your standard paper grade has a contrast range of 0.8 or 6.3 : 1, the problem will be quite different if you print the same negative. If you expose to produce a minimum tone from the maximum density area of the negative, a full black will be produced by the negative density equal to the maximum density of the negative minus the contrast scale of the paper. This means that all negative densities between 0.8 and 0.6 will reproduce as full black; and as these correspond

51 A test strip made to determine correct printing exposure

to the shadow detail in the negative, the print will have clogged shadows. On the other hand, if you expose for a full black from the minimum density area of the negative, all densities between 1.4 and 1.6 in the negative will reproduce clear white in the print, and as these correspond to highlight detail, the print will have burnt out highlights. In both cases the print will appear too contrasty.

Ideally you should choose a paper with a contrast scale the same as the negative density range (in the case of our example, 1.0 or 10 : 1). In this case all detail in the negative from delicate highlights to the deepest shadow detail will be correctly reproduced.

When you have had some experience of printing, you will find that it is possible to choose the correct grade of paper merely by looking at the negative and making a comparison – either real or mental – with other similar negatives from which you have already made good prints. However, if you have an enlarger exposure meter you can choose your paper grade with much more accuracy by measuring the effective density range of each negative in much the same way as you measure the brightness range of a subject. The way to do this is to place the probe of the meter in the area of deepest shadow in which you want detail on the projected image, and adjust the

enlarger lens aperture until the meter reads 1 second. Next move the probe into the brightest highlight in which detail is required; the reading on the meter now indicates the density range of the negative as a ratio. For example, if the highlight reading is 12 seconds, the negative density range is 12 : 1. If you cannot reduce the shadow reading to 1 second, it is quite in order to set it at any other figure, but in this case you must divide the highlight reading by the shadow reading. For instance, if the shadow reading is 3 seconds and the highlight reading is 30 seconds the negative density range is 30/3 = 10 : 1. When you have measured the negative density range, choose a grade of paper that has a contrast scale as close as possible from Table 4.

Table 4   Paper Contrast Scales

Kodak Bromide

Grade 0	1.50	(32 : 1)
1	1.35	(22 : 1)
2	1.2	(16 : 1)
3	1.05	(11 : 1)
4	0.75	(5.6 : 1)

Ilford Ilfobrom

Grade 0	1.6	(40 : 1)
1	1.4	(25 : 1)
2	1.2	(16 : 1)
3	1.0	(10 : 1)
4	0.8	(6.3 : 1)
5	0.6	(4 : 1)

Exposure determination

The next step is to determine the correct printing exposure, and there are two ways of doing this. You can use the old test-strip method or you can use one of the many enlarger exposure meters that are now available on the market. These instruments will save you a great deal of time and material, and I would advise you to consider one almost as soon as you start printing. But first let us consider test strips.

Test strips are simply small prints made by exposing the paper in steps, each step receiving twice the exposure of the preceding step (Illus 51). When you have developed, fixed and washed the test strip, decide which step gives you the results nearest to what you want. Then make a second test strip, this time just covering the step either side of the one you have chosen and with, say, 2 seconds difference between steps. This should then give you an accurate indication of the correct exposure to use. Kodak make a device called an Enlarger Exposure Guide, which takes the form of a circular step wedge to simplify making test strips; you place this on a piece of printing paper on your enlarger base-board and expose it for 1 minute. The grey steps cut down the light to give a series of steps equivalent to exposures ranging from 2 to 48 seconds.

Although test strips will give you perfectly exposed prints every time, they do consume rather a lot of valuable time and material, and, in my opinion, the cost of an enlarger exposure meter is well justified. Some take a reading from a small area on the negative and some integrate all the tones on the whole negative. Which you choose is largely a matter of personal preference, and their operating principle is basically the same. After calibrating the meter by making a print by the test-strip method, you set up the meter to give a reading the same as the exposure determined. For all other negatives it is then simply a matter of measuring a suitable area of the negative and giving the indicated exposure. Full instructions are supplied with all meters, so I do not propose to go into the matter further here. One thing to watch, though, if you use an integrating meter, is to mask off any clear area of rebate around the negative so that it does not affect the reading and give you under-exposed prints. Turn off your safelight when you take the reading, or this may cause a false indication, since the CdS cells used in these meters are particularly sensitive to the red end of the spectrum.

Dodging When you are making the print exposure, you can carry out a certain amount of corrective work on the tones you want in the finished print. Called dodging, this is done by shading a small part of the image so that part of the paper receives less exposure than the rest and the tone produced is therefore lighter than it would be in a straight print. Alternatively you can shade all the image except a small part, so that the corresponding area of the print is darker in tone than it would have been.

Many workers use their hands for this shading work (it is called holding back when you shade a small portion, and burning in when you leave just a small area unshaded), but it takes a little practice to be able to form the shadows just where you want them and nowhere else. To start with, at least, a selection of small pieces of shaped black cards on wire holders are useful for holding back and larger pieces of card with holes cut in them for burning in. But whether you use dodging tools of this sort or your hands, remember to keep them constantly moving to avoid producing hard edges to your shading.

Correcting distortion As I said before, if you tilt the camera up or down when taking a picture, the negative will show vertical lines converging at the top or bottom. You can correct this at the printing stage quite easily (Illus 52, 53). All you do is tilt the printing paper on the enlarger base-board by the same amount as you tilted the camera when taking the picture, but in the opposite direction. What happens is that the part of the paper at the highest point receives a smaller degree of magnification than the rest of the sheet, so the verticals become truly vertical again. But you will have to stop the enlarger lens down well to give sufficient depth of focus to ensure that the whole of the image is sharp. Focus about a third of the way across the paper from the highest point, and stop down until the whole image appears sharp. Then give it another stop for good measure.

As well as stopping the lens down well, you will have to graduate the exposure somewhat, because the part of the paper nearest the lens (at the highest point) will receive more exposure than the rest of the sheet. So shade the print progressively for part of the exposure; the exact amount you can only find out by trial and error.

When the camera has been tilted during exposure:
52 The converging verticals can be corrected

Processing the print

Developing It is just as important to develop printing papers properly as it is to develop films properly. In fact, in many ways it is even more important, because the print is the finished product of your photography and there is not all that much you can do to it after processing to correct mistakes or faults. Just because you can see the image forming as you develop the print is no excuse for grossly under- or over-developing if you find you have given the wrong exposure. Papers are designed to give their ultimate quality when developed for $1\frac{1}{2}$–2 minutes at 20°C (68°F). it is usually possible to push the development time by a minute or so without losing too much quality, but if you try to cut it, you will almost certainly end up with muddy prints.

There is a wide range of developers on the market, all of which are suitable for any make of paper, and they all produce good image colours and a range of tones more or less the same as the developer recommended by the paper manufacturer. For emergencies it is worth keeping a bottle each of a high contrast and soft gradation developer in your darkroom. You can use these to increase or decrease the contrast scale of the paper by roughly one grade, and they can provide an extra creative control in your print making.

Stop, fix, and wash After development of the print is complete, it is important to stop the action of the developer quickly in just the same way as when processing negatives, and in fact, the same stop-bath solution (2 per cent acetic acid) can be used. The immersion time in this bath should be about 1 minute.

Fixing completes the chemical treatment of the print, and can be carried out in any of the proprietary fixers on the market. It is worth noting, however, that the use of rapid fixer for prints is rather uneconomical: while a rapid fixer will complete its work in about 2 minutes or so and a conventional fixer takes 8–10 minutes, the difference in these times is of little significance when you consider that you have to wash the prints for anything up to an hour afterwards.

After fixing, the prints must be thoroughly washed to remove all traces of chemicals from the emulsion and the paper base. This takes *at least* 30 minutes in running water and preferably 45 minutes to an hour. Any chemicals left in the print may lie dormant for a long time, only to manifest themselves in the form of stains perhaps years later. When I make large prints for display purposes, I usually treat them in a proprietary hypo eliminator after a brief rinse and then wash them for a further 10 minutes or so. This seems to work, as no stained prints have been produced by this method so far.

Print finishing

When your prints are dry – you can dry them naturally by hanging them up or laying them out on sheets of newspaper, face up, or you can dry them on a heated print dryer – there are just two jobs to do to make the prints suitable for display – spotting and mounting.

Spotting is the removal of those small white spots that inevitably appear on almost every print you make. To get rid of them, you need one or two very fine artists' paint brushes and a tube each of black and sepia watercolour. Mix up the colour to the right tone and apply it with a light dabbing action. Start with the spots in the darker areas and gradually work through to the lighter areas, adding extra water as you go to lighten the tone of the watercolours. Black spots are best removed by gently scraping with an extremely sharp knife.

There are several methods of mounting prints, of which dry mounting is without doubt the best. If you use dry-mounting tissue, you really need a special dry-mounting press or iron, but there is a product on the market that makes the job simple with just a domestic iron. It is called Paterson Dry Mounting solution and is a lacquer you paint on the back of the print. When it is dry, you simply position the print on the mount, cover it with a sheet of clean dry paper and iron it on with a domestic iron.

Dry-mounting tissue is a little more tricky to use. First you need to tack it on to the back of the print and trim both the print and the tissue to the right size. Then you must position the print on the mount and tack it in place. Finally place the print in the mounting press with a sheet of clean dry paper on top of it and apply heat and pressure for about a minute. The boards on which you mount your prints must be of good quality; some cheaper boards contain impurities which, over a period of years can cause staining of the print. Most photographers seem to use white or cream mounts because that is what has always been used, but there is a growing trend these days towards using grey or brown mounts. These colours show off the prints better, in my opinion. I nearly always use either a fairly dark grey or, if the prints are warm tone, a dark buff or light brown.

Appendices

1 Filters, their effects and factors

Filter	Factor	Effect
Yellow	×2–×3	Lightens yellows, darkens blues. Makes clouds stand out against a slightly darkened sky. Absorbs UV slightly.
Yellow-green	×2	Similar to yellow, but improves rendering of greens in landscapes. Useful for outdoor portraits.
Green	×2–×3	Lightens greens and emphasises detail and texture in leaves, etc. Absorbs UV slightly; darkens orange and red. Darkens sun-tan but emphasises freckles.
Orange	×4	Gives dramatic cloud effects by darkening blue sky. Eliminates UV, so cutting through haze. Gives good textural effects in brick and stonework, and emphasises detail and texture in dark wood. Darkens green.
Red	×8	Produces exaggerated cloud effects and spectacular sunsets. Eliminates haze and produces strong contrast for architectural studies.
Blue	×2	Improves skin tones in portraits taken by artificial light. Emphasises detail in shadows lit by blue skylight. Exaggerates haze, darkens red.
Polarising	×2–×4	Minimises reflections from reflective non-metallic surfaces. Darkens sky without affecting otther colours, so can be used with colour film.

2 Light-source colour temperatures

Daylight sources	°K	Mireds
Average daylight sun plus cloud ranges from	6,500	154
to	5,500	182
Direct sunlight		
Summer 10am–3pm	5,800	172
after 3pm	5,000	200
after 4.30pm	4,750	210
Two hours after sunrise	4,400	227
One hour after sunrise	3,500	286
Daylight with obscured sun		
Very clear blue sky, in shade	26,000	38
Clear blue sky, in shade	19,000	52
Average blue sky, in shade	16,000	62
Blue sky with thin white cloud	13,000	77
Cloudy blue sky with shade	8,900	112
Cloudy sky with light shade	8,000	125
Overcast sky	7,000	143

Artificial light sources	°K	Mireds
Household lamps under 100W	2,800	357
over 100W	2,900	345
Studio tungsten floodlamps	3,000	333
500W over-run bulbs Type B	3,200	312
Photoflood bulbs	3,400	294
Tungsten halogen lamps	3,300	303
Fluorescent tubes, Warmlite	3,500	286
Clear flash bulbs	3,800	263
Fluorescent tubes, Daylight	5,000	200
Blue flash bulbs	5,500	182
Average electronic flash	6,000	167

3 Filters for colour photography

Filter	Mired shift	Factor	Effect
R1½	+15	×1¼	Prevents blue cast by strongly absorbing ultra-violet in blue daylight and light shadow. Also for use with daylight films and electronic flash.
R3	+30	×1¼	Prevents strong blue cast especially at mid-day and caused by wide expanses of blue sky, blue seascapes or strong shadows.
R6	+60	×1½	For use in intense blue day-light and shade.
R12	+120	×2	For using artificial light film in daylight.
B1½	−15	×1¼	To prevent general reddish cast caused by clear sunlight before 10am and after 3pm in summer. Eliminates over-red flesh tones.
B3	−30	×1½	Prevents general red cast caused by clear sunlight before 9am and after 4pm in summer.
B6	−60	×2	Prevents strong red casts from sunsets.
B12	−120	×4	For using daylight film in artificial light.

4 Reciprocity failure corrections

Indicated-exp (seconds)	Corrected exp (neg materials) to nearest ½sec	Corrected exp (rev materials) to nearest ½sec
1½	1½	2
2	3	2½
3	4½	4
4	6½	6
5	8½	7½
6	11	9½
7	13	11
8	16	13
9	19	15
10	22	17½
12	27	22
15	35	30
18	43	36
20	50	42
25	66	55
30	85	69
35	103	88
40	124	104
45	144	122
50	164	140
55	187	160
60	210	180
70	270	225
80	300	265
90	360	314
120	510	455

5 Close-up tables

Table 1 Focusing Distances for Supplementary Close-up Lenses

Supp lens	Camera set to (ft)	Subject distance (in)	Reproduction scale approx (:1 reduction) for 50mm lens
+ 1 dioptre	Infinity	39	20
(1m focal length)	20	34	17
	10	30	15
	5	23¾	11.7
	3	18¾	9
	2	14¾	6.9
+ 2 dioptre	Infinity	19⅝	10
(500mm focal length)	20	18¼	9.2
	10	17	8.5
	5	15	7.3
	3	12½	6
	2	10½	4.9
+ 3 dioptre	Infinity	13	6.65
(333mm focal length)	20	12½	6.37
	10	12	6
	5	10¾	5.28
	3	9½	4.55
	2	8¼	3.82
+ 4 dioptre	Infinity	9½	5
(250mm focal length)	20	9¼	4.64
	10	9	4.48
	5	8½	4.18
	3	7½	3.56
	2	7	3.26
+ 5 dioptre	Infinity	7⅞	4
(200mm focal length)	20	7½	3.76
	10	7¼	3.61
	5	7	3.44
	3	6¾	3.28
	2	6⅜	3.05

The subject distances quoted remain constant irrespective of the focal length of the camera lens used. Reproduction scale varies according to the focal length of the camera lens. The focal-length figures quoted are for a 50mm lens.

Table 2 Equivalent Focal Lengths for 50mm Camera lens

Supp lens (dioptres)	Focal length	Equivalent power (dioptres)	Equivalent focal length
+ 1	1 metre	+ 21	47.62mm
+ 2	500mm	+ 22	45.45mm
+ 3	333mm	+ 23	43.48mm
+ 4	250mm	+ 24	41.67mm
+ 5	200mm	+ 25	40.00mm
+ 6	167mm	+ 26	38.46mm
+ 7	143mm	+ 27	37.00mm
+ 8	125mm	+ 28	35.71mm
+ 9	111mm	+ 29	34.48mm
+ 10	100mm	+ 30	33.33mm

Table 3 Reproduction Ratios with Lenses of Various Focal Lengths

Extension (mm)	Reproduction ratio (35mm)	Reproduction ratio (50mm)	Reproduction ratio (90mm)	Reproduction ratio (135mm)
10	1:3.5	1:5	1:9	1:13.5
15	1:2.28	1:3.33	1:6	1:9
20	1:1.75	1:2.5	1:4.5	1:6.75
25	1:1.4	1:2	1:3.6	1:5.4
30	1:1.17	1:1.67	1:3	1:4.5
35	1:1	1:1.43	1:2.57	1:3.86
40	1.14:1	1:1.25	1:2.25	1:3.38
45	1.285:1	1:1.11	1:2	1:3
50	1.43:1	1:1	1:1.8	1:2.7
55	1.57:1	1.1:1	1:1.64	1:2.46
60	1.71:1	1.2:1	1:1.5	1:2.25
65	1.855:1	1.3:1	1:1.385	1:2.08
70	2:1	1.4:1	1:1.285	1:1.93
75	2.14:1	1.5:1	1:1.2	1:1.8
80	2.28:1	1.6:1	1:1.125	1:1.69
85	2.4:1	1.7:1	1:1.06	1:1.59
90	2.57:1	1.8:1	1:1	1:1.5
95	2.71:1	1.9:1	1.055:1	1:1.42
100	2.86:1	2:1	1.11:1	1:1.35
105	3:1	2.1:1	1.17:1	1:1.285
110	3.14:1	2.2:1	1.122:1	1:1.23
115	3.29:1	2.3:1	1.28:1	1:1.17
120	3.43:1	2.4:1	1.33:1	1:1.125

Table 4 Exposure increases for Various Reproduction Ratios

Reproduction ratio	Exposure correction factor	Approx exposure increase (stops)
1:20	1.1	–
1:15	1.12	–
1:10	1.2	1/3
1:8	1.26	1/3
1:6	1.34	1/3
1:5	1.44	2/3
1:4	1.56	2/3
1:3	1.77	2/3
1:2	2.25	1
1:1	4	2
2:1	9	3
3:1	16	4
4:1	25	$4\frac{2}{3}$
5:1	36	5
6:1	49	$5\frac{2}{3}$
8:1	81	$6\frac{1}{3}$
10:1	121	$6\frac{2}{3}$
15:1	256	8
20:1	441	$8\frac{2}{3}$

Bibliography

Adams, Ansel. *Camera and Lens* (New York, 1970)
——. *The Negative* (New York, revised ed, 1966)
——. *The Print* (New York, 1950)
Berger, Heinz. *Agfacolor* (Wuppertal, 1967)
Feininger, Andreas. *Principles of Composition in Photography* (1973)
——. *Basic Colour Photography* (1972)
Gaunt, Leonard. *The Praktica Way* (London, 1972)
Life Library of Photography. *The Camera* (Amsterdam, 1971)
——. *Color* (Amsterdam, 1973)
——. *Light and Film* (Amsterdam, 1972)
——. *The Print* (Amsterdam, 1972)
Watkins, Derek, *Practical Photographic Enlarging* (Newton Abbot, 1973)
——. *Good Photography Made Easy* (Newton Abbot, 1975)

Acknowledgements

I would like first of all to thank CZ Scientific Instruments for their invaluable help in lending me several Pentacon, Zeiss and Sigma lenses and other accessories for my Praktica cameras. These enabled me to illustrate points that I would otherwise not have been able to. In particular I would like to thank Terry Hill of CZ for organising this for me. Other companies and individuals who have given me enormous help in producing this book are, in alphabetical order: Agfa-Gevaert Limited, Group I & E Limited, Ilford Limited, JR Distributing Company, Kodak Limited, Paterson Products Limited, Sandra Price, Rank Audio Visual Limited, and Tony Ridge.

Finally I would like to thank my wife Jill who, as always, was patient, understanding and sympathetic. She also offered much valuable constructive criticism.

Index